THE

# moolala

GUIDE TO ROCKIN'
YOUR RRSP

———

# BRUCE SELLERY

# THE
# moolala
## GUIDE TO
## ROCKIN'
## YOUR RRSP

FIGURE **1** PUBLISHING  *Vancouver*

Cataloguing data available from Library and Archives Canada
ISBN 978-1-927958-00-1 (pbk.)
ISBN 978-1-9921586-0-6 (ebook)

Cover and text design by Peter Cocking
Cover photograph by David Cooper
Printed and bound in Canada by Friesens

Parts of this book were first published on MoneySense.ca
and in *Moolala* (McClelland & Stewart, 2011).

Figure 1 Publishing Inc.
Vancouver BC Canada
www.figure1pub.com

*This book is dedicated to my Mom and Dad.*

*I am endlessly grateful for your
wisdom, support, and unconditional love.*

---

# CONTENTS

■>■>■>■>■

**STEP FOUR:** TAKE ACTION

■>■>■>■>■

**STEP FIVE:** STAY ENGAGED

# INTRODUCTION

---

**T**HE SUN was setting across a spectacular mountain range in Patagonia. My mom and I had just finished another stunning day of trekking up and down rocky paths, across glaciers, and through streams. She was 70 years old at the time, fit in body, sharp in mind, and full of the spirit of adventure. This was by no means her first big trek. She had started with Gokyo Ri in Nepal at the age of 50, and she followed that with trips to Peru, Tibet, France, and China.

There we were, mother and son, a million miles from anywhere, crouched in our little tent getting ready for dinner as darkness fell. I can't remember what the catalyst was, but for some reason both of us fell into uncontrollable fits of laughter—the kind that hurts your belly and is impossible to stop. The best kind of laughter there is.

This guide is not about belly laughs, or travelling around South America. It is about retirement savings. The fact is that most of us would rather talk about almost *anything* other than retirement savings. The mere mention of the topic makes most people feel worried, anxious, despondent, or annoyed. And yet you have this sense that you *should* talk about it, that you could be doing more to set up your 80-year-old self for success. What I want to highlight with my brief South America story is that my mom and I were able to take this trip at all. We could take it because she could afford her share.

My mom had worked hard her whole life—raising five kids with my dad, working outside the home as a pharmacist, and finding her feet again after my parents divorced. She made tough choices about money—how to earn it and where to spend it. And that afforded her the freedom to go on a hiking trip with her youngest son in Patagonia.

I want that same freedom when I'm her age. My daughter, Abby, is just 4 years old now, but when she is an adult, and if she is willing, I'd like to go trekking with her too. I want to be sure that I'm financially able to do what I want until I'm no longer physically able. To do that I know I'll need to be smart about my money. And that is what this guide is about.

### Why I Wrote This Guide

My mission in life is to inspire people to get a handle on their money so they can live the lives they want. That is why I wrote my first book, *Moolala: Why Smart People Do Dumb Things with Their Money (and What You Can Do About It)*. That book was about helping smart people gain the knowledge, skills, and habits they need to start doing smart things with their money more often. Many of the book's topics resonated with people, but retirement savings was one area in particular where readers said they wanted more support. There is certainly no shortage of information out there about Registered Retirement Savings Plans—mountains of it, in fact. And still, most people I talk to have mixed feelings about retirement savings. Here are a few examples:

> **My mission in life is to inspire people to get a handle on their money so they can live the lives they want.**

*"I feel frustrated and perplexed. It isn't like I splurge at the mall every weekend. I know I should be saving more, but I just can't seem to find a way given all the demands on my money—the mortgage, car payments, the kids. How do other people manage to do it?"*
—Cheryl, 38, stay-at-home mom. Married with three kids.

*"I hardly think about it—and then I panic and feel like I'm not doing enough. I feel behind and don't think I'll ever be able to retire. I'm already 46 and only have about $10,000 in my RRSPs. How will I ever be able to save enough?"*

—Heather, 46, retail manager. Single.

*"I generally feel secure. As a 40-something, I think to myself, 'wow, retirement is no longer this far-off conceptual thing, but something that is real and tangible that now requires active planning.'"*

—Michael, 42, consultant. Married with one child.

*"I feel totally unclear. I don't have any 'vision' for what retirement looks like—where will I be, what will I be doing, how long will I live and how much money will I need for it."*

—Marie, 45, arts administrator. Single.

*"I feel bored and depressed. It's totally a 'should.' I know I should be putting away more per month but there's never enough ... plus we want to enjoy life now too. Socking money away for some distant future is no fun at all."*

—Maya, 45, technical writer. Married with two kids.

*"I feel resistant. Both my parents died young—age 48 and 63—and I resist saving because a part of me thinks, 'what's the point?'"*

—McKenna, 40, writer. Married with one child.

*"I feel pretty good at the moment. I put away a significant chunk of money and max out my RRSP and TFSA each year. Yet I look at my statements, and they don't seem to be increasing in value. Besides that, I really don't know how much is enough."*

—Carolyn, 43, HR consultant. Married with one child.

In a word or two, how do you feel about retirement savings? Confident, optimistic, secure, worried, irritated, confused? I find that it is helpful to identify where you're at right now in this moment, before we start getting into the details.

When I think about retirement savings I feel _____.

You feel however you feel, right? But I wanted to write a guide that made people feel better about retirement savings by inspiring them to develop a plan and then go out and take action on that plan. The result is what you are holding in your hands.

## Why Read the Moolala Guide To Rockin' Your RRSP

I'm asking you to invest the money it will cost to buy this guide, plus your time and energy to work through it. So what will you get out of it? You will receive three really great benefits if you work your way through this guide:

### Retirement savings will become relevant to you and your life

Identifying why it is in your self-interest to contribute to a Registered Retirement Savings Plan is job one. It isn't enough that your dad keeps droning on about the importance of retirement savings (or the banks, or the finance minister, or even me for that matter). Most people's eyes glaze over when the topic comes up—in part because it can be dreadfully boring and in part because it feels like the pundits and proselytizers are talking to someone else. But I am not talking to someone else. I am talking to you. And I am going to do my darndest to make retirement savings relevant to you, your family, and your life.

### You'll develop a simple plan to rock your RRSP immediately

You might not have an RRSP set up yet—you might not have gotten around to it, or you might not be convinced an RRSP is the best way to go. Or you might have one set up, but you're pretty sure there is more you could be doing to make the most of it. Whatever your circumstances are, I am going to help you develop a simple plan to take you from where you are today to where you want to be in the future.

### You'll be inspired to get off your duff and take action

There is a big difference between knowing what to do and actually going out and doing it. Sure, you need a certain amount of knowledge to get a handle on your money. But way, way, way more important than amassing lots of knowledge is taking action. This *Moolala Guide to Rockin' Your* RRSP will focus on giving you everything you need to be inspired to get off your duff and take action.

I've drawn on a large group of people to help on this front. I call them the Moolala Community and they are people like you from across Canada who have generously agreed to offer their insights on the good, bad, and ugly of their retirement savings. The idea is that their stories will help you identify some insights of your own. I have also included "Q & A" sections throughout. These are real questions from real people and they are intended to address broad retirement savings topics in more detail.

. . . . . . . . . . . . .

**There is a big difference between knowing what to do and actually going out and doing it.**

. . . . . . . . . . . . .

## What the Moolala Method Is All About: Knowledge, Skills, and Habits

Getting a handle on your retirement savings is a function of three things: knowledge, skills, and habits. You need some basic knowledge about personal finance, taxes, and investing; you need a few skills to be able to do the right things; and you need to develop a habit of doing those things consistently over time.

Think about your health for a second. You can know what broccoli is and the great nutrients it contains, like vitamin C and calcium. But that *knowledge* isn't enough. You need the basic *skills* to prepare the broccoli. No Martha Stewart flourish is required—you can simply cut up the broccoli, then steam, drain, and serve it with a little salt and butter. You now have some knowledge and some skills, but in order to eat healthily over time you need to get into the *habit* of buying and serving broccoli every once in a while.

You may never love broccoli. And you may never love the topic of retirement savings either. But gaining knowledge, developing skills, and ingraining good habits in both areas can make a big difference in the quality of your life.

## The Five Steps of the Moolala Method

The Moolala Method is the way to gain knowledge, develop skills, and ingrain habits so you can get a handle on your retirement savings. It is made up of five simple steps that will take you from where you are today to where you want to be in the future. This method was introduced in my first book, *Moolala*. That book was a wide-ranging look at personal finance, but the five-step method also works for retirement savings, a topic that we just touched on in *Moolala*. On occasion I have used material from the first book and built on it with new examples and insights specific to the topic of retirement savings.

Now, to the five steps themselves:

### Step 1: Lay the foundation

In the first step of the Moolala Method, we'll focus on laying a foundation of knowledge. Of course that includes the basics of the RRSP and an overview of how to develop a simple plan, but it also includes gaining knowledge about the realities of retirement these days and knowledge about your own wants and needs when it comes to your retirement.

I bet you're a smart person. And what I know about smart people is that very often we do dumb things with our money. I definitely fit into this category and my hunch is that you do too. We will look at why this happens to so many of us and what you can do to become a smart person who does smart things with your money a little more often.

Specifically, we'll look at your strengths and weaknesses when it comes to retirement savings and at what gets you excited when you think about life after your working days are done. Remember that retirement is a life stage, not an activity. You can't actually "do" retirement; you do "things" in retirement and those things cost money. Thinking about the activities that you'll want to do during your retirement—as far away as that may be—will give you a sense of what your future life will cost—and how much you need to save for it. It will also give you the inspiration to save for retirement, especially when you'd really rather put the money into a great night out with friends, kids' hockey equipment, or a few takeout meals to ease the burden of family life. In all likelihood you will need to make trade-offs, and knowing why you're making them will make a big difference.

Now, if you are still a few decades away from retirement you might think I'm a nutcase for even suggesting you think about all this now. But trust me. It is worth it.

> I bet you're a smart person. And what I know about smart people is that very often we do dumb things with our money. I definitely fit into this category and my hunch is that you do too.

**Step 2: Determine how much you need**

Now that the foundation is laid, you can start to think about how much money you will need in order to get you what you want when you are no longer working. The math isn't hard to do—and yet most people don't know how big their nest egg will need to be. Why? Because it is scary. It feels easier to remain oblivious than to address the reality of how much you'll need to save to retire.

While it might be easier, being oblivious isn't very helpful when it comes to getting your retirement savings on track. Better to know that nest egg number so you can actually do something about it. In Step 2 of the Moolala Method we will determine how much money you will need at retirement, point out the pitfalls to avoid, and address some of the fears about that number that may come up along the way.

**Step 3: Develop the plan**

Once you have a sense of what you want for your retirement and how much you need to save for it, the Moolala Method will help you develop a simple plan to reach your goal. The plan will cover a number of different areas, depending on your own unique circumstances, and answer many of the most common questions people have about retirement savings. We are aiming to come up with the simplest plan possible—no binders or fancy software or massive to-do lists, just a few key actions that will give you the biggest bang for your buck.

### Step 4: Take action

Now that you've developed a basic plan, it's time to take action. You'll be ahead of most people on your block just by having a plan to begin with, and this step focuses on giving you the skills to move that plan from your notebook (or napkin) into your real life. I'll reveal the four ingredients that action requires and provide you with a few super simple actions to give you momentum.

### Step 5: Stay engaged

The final step of the Moolala Method is about staying engaged with the plan. We'll look at the most important habits to foster and how you can "set it and forget it," so you can continue to save while spending very little time working on your retirement savings and lots of time on the things you love about life. And for you "list" people, this step includes a checklist of everything there is to do to get a handle on your retirement savings. For you "non-list" people, saying I have no idea what he's talking about, let's just go with the flow.

## Let's Go Trekking

Wherever you're at, however you're feeling, and whatever amount you have already saved or not saved for your retirement, I know you can rock your RRSP. Why am I so confident? Because over the years I have seen so many examples of people who had absolutely no knowledge, crumby skills, and very bad habits take action to get a handle on their retirement savings. If these people can do it, anyone can.

Slip on your backpack and tie up your boots. It is time to go trekking.

# STEP 1

---

## LAY THE
## FOUNDATION

# { 1 }

## WHY SMART PEOPLE DO DUMB
## THINGS WITH THEIR MONEY
### DEAL WITH THE MYTHS AND
### MISCONCEPTIONS OF RRSPS

---

I AM NOT a patient person. Our tech-addled world has become incredibly fast-paced and yet I still growl impatiently at my smartphone when it takes a millisecond to update itself. In fact, a friend once suggested that I take "patience pills," which I thought was a brilliant idea until I learned that no such chemical intervention existed.

I bet some of you are like me, anxiously tapping your feet, desperate to flip past this section as time ticks down to the RRSP deadline. I understand. I really do. But I'm going to ask you to take a metaphorical patience pill. The who, what, where, when, why, and how of RRSPS are coming, don't you worry. Before we get to the basics of RRSPS it is really important to ensure that you have the necessary knowledge about two other important areas—knowledge of what retirement, twenty-first-century-style, will look like, and knowledge of your own wants and needs about your retirement, as well as the factors that may be preventing you from getting a handle on your money.

## Retirement, Twenty-First-Century Style

My grandparents on my dad's side had a pretty simple retirement consisting of regular bridge games, afternoon naps, a devotion to *Reader's Digest*, and a nice glass of sherry enjoyed every evening at cocktail hour. This is not the retirement of my parents, and it certainly isn't going to be my retirement either. Why? Because the world has changed in some very significant ways. You and I are going to live longer, more active lives than our grandparents did. Good news, I say, but that means that we will need to save more money to fund a longer retirement.

We also have more expensive tastes today when it comes to technology, real estate, cars, and international travel. My grandparents— who lived through two world wars and the Great Depression—would have a hard time imagining the existence of luxuries we now call necessities. Case in point: the smartphone was unfathomable in the seventies and is somehow indispensable today. You can debate how necessary all this spending is—including second degrees, second cars, second homes and second marriages—but the fact is we're forking out cash hand over fist. And quite often we fund this largesse with credit cards, developing a tolerance for debt levels that would have sent Granny and Grandpops to the asylum. To top it all off, our longer, more expensive lives come at a time when full-time staff jobs have become scarce, and generous pension plans even scarcer.

> The Registered Retirement Savings Plan (RRSP) provides a nice tax break and a huge incentive to save, but most Canadians still don't take full advantage of it.

There is a fairly short list of retirement savings vehicles to choose from. The RRSP is the one that you have probably heard the most about—and for good reason. It has been around the longest, is the most common, and it is the best option for most Canadians.

The Registered Retirement Savings Plan (RRSP) provides a nice tax break and a huge incentive to save, but most Canadians still don't take full advantage of it. In fact, according to Statistics Canada, just 24% of people who filed their income taxes in 2011 made a contribution to RRSPs, and the average amount of that contribution was just $2,830—barely enough to pay for your hydro bill in retirement, let alone fund the fantasy of "Freedom 55."

To sum up: you and I are going to live longer and want to spend more. But our jobs will be less secure, our pensions non-existent, and the best retirement savings vehicle we've got—the RRSP—will just sit there, rusting away in the metaphoric parking lot. That is, unless we wake up to the fact that the responsibility to learn more about the new realities of retirement and to save for our own retirement rests squarely on our shoulders.

## Myths and Misconceptions

We have done an abysmal job of educating Canadians about personal finance. No surprise then that there are a lot of myths and misconceptions out there about retirement savings and RRSPs in particular. Let's address a few of them right now.

- **"The government will cover the basics"**

  I guess it depends on what you consider the basics. We'll talk in detail in chapter 5 about what you can expect from the Canada Pension Plan and Old Age Security, but it amounts to only about $1,000 per person per month on average. Think about your cash burn today—how far would $1,000 take you? And you will likely have additional health care expenses as you age, and the cost of home care, physiotherapy, elective medical procedures, and some prescription drugs may come out of your own pocket. You may live a longer and more active life, but your enjoyment of that life might be curtailed because of your inability to pay for it.

- **"I can't afford to save for retirement right now"**

  The cost of living today is very high, especially when you factor in housing costs. I hear the "I can't afford it" complaint all the time and from people at all income levels. But it isn't about affordability. It's about trade-offs. We are constantly trading off time, energy, convenience, pleasure, and money. It is just that we are unaware that we are making these trade-offs. If you can't afford to save for retirement now, I can tell you it isn't going to be much easier in ten or fifteen years. Sure, your kids might not be raiding your wallet with the same frequency, and you might be making more money, but by then you won't have time on your side, so you'll have to save a lot more. In effect, by not saving now, you're stealing money from your future self. Picture someone in your life who is, say, 80 years old. How different would his life be right now if his retirement income was cut in half?

- **"I'll just work longer"**
  There are many occupations where you could work full- or part-time beyond the typical age of retirement, especially if your skills are in high demand or if you work for yourself. But in many other fields, it may not be possible to work into your eighties, either because you won't have the physical or mental strength to do the job or because the industry is reticent to employ older workers. You can bemoan the prejudice inherent in this second point, but I'm not banking on ageism's disappearance in my lifetime. My main issue with a plan to simply work longer—over and above the reality that it might not be possible—is that it takes away your freedom to stop working when you want to.

- **"My family will provide for me"**
  You may come from a family in which an inheritance is likely. But can you bank on it? If you think that an inheritance is in your future, sure, it is relevant to your retirement savings. But you'll want to get more details on what that inheritance is likely to look like. While it is a delicate conversation, it is one worth having with those from whom you might inherit. The ballpark amount could be more than you expect, but it could also be less, and if so it is much better to know that now instead of in twenty years,

when you'll have less time to save. And be realistic about the chance of your not receiving that money from your aging relative: an extended stay in an expensive private retirement home, a re-marriage, investment losses, or the relative simply living a really long time can cut into the amount you end up receiving.

You may also think that your kids will provide a retirement cushion, either in the form of a stipend or free room and board. Again, it is worth checking those assumptions, as they simply may not be accurate. And consider a backup plan in case life changes for your kids—for example, they move to another city and you don't want to follow them, or they have financial hardships of their own that prevent them from helping you.

- **"My retirement plan is simple: I won't need much"**
  What does "simple" mean to you? Take this reader who said, "I'm not very ambitious. I just want to be able to do the same things I like doing now, only more of them." In this case those things include world travel, eating out, and living in a big house in an urban centre. This kind of retirement might not seem ambitious, but depending on how much you will have saved, it could be very ambitious to think that you'll be able to replicate your current level of income in retirement.

  If, however, your version of "simple" is downsizing to a smaller home in a cheaper real estate market and limiting your spending on travel and entertainment, you may be able to say with confidence that you won't need much. We will address this question in much more detail in chapter 5.

  > Your house doesn't make for much of a retirement plan. That's because in order to use your house for that purpose you will need to sell it.

- **"My house is my retirement plan"**
  Your house probably represents a big portion of both your monthly expenses and total net worth, but it doesn't make for much of a retirement plan. That's because in order to use your

house for that purpose you will need to sell it. Why? Because you can't eat your house. You will need to unlock some of the equity you have built up over the years to put groceries in your fridge. That might seem like a good idea in theory now, but it can be a tough one emotionally to follow through on. For example, downsizing in square footage doesn't always mean downsizing in price—a downtown condo can cost as much as a house in the suburbs.

There are other ways to pull out equity from your house, including a reverse mortgage or a home equity line of credit. But the costs associated with both these options can be prohibitive. And if you need money fast—to replace a car or deal with an unexpected medical expense, for example—it can be hard to get at because a house is not very liquid. It is much easier to own investments that you can sell to give you the cash flow you need.

- **"RRSPs are a scam"**

 Over the last decade the newspapers have been full of stories about Ponzi schemes, crooked investment "advisers," and insider trading. That has led some people to fear the RRSP itself. This is a mistake.

 An RRSP is just a special kind of account that shelters some of your income from the tax collectors. As we'll discuss in chapter 12, the quality of the investments you buy to put in to that account can vary widely, but to say that RRSPs themselves are a scam simply isn't accurate. You are confusing a type of account with investments that could go into that account. RRSPs themselves are not a scam. In fact, I'd argue that RRSPs are one of the few perks that the average taxpayer has left. Sure, you need to pay attention to where you put your money to ensure that you aren't being taken for a ride, but don't do yourself the disservice of letting fear push you off course.

The myths and misconceptions outlined here partly explain why most people have such dismal retirement savings. A second major explanation comes from a lack of self-knowledge—not knowing your own wants and needs when it comes to your retirement or what factors might be preventing you from getting a handle on your retirement savings. I am going to do my best to improve your financial knowledge right now.

## Hello, My Name Is _____. (Getting To Know Yourself)

Let's focus on you for a minute: your life, your circumstances, and, in particular, your strengths and weaknesses.

As I mentioned, smart, capable people do dumb things with their money. Being smart can make you successful at school, your job, perhaps even in your relationships, but it isn't enough to ensure that you're successful at handling your retirement savings. As smart and capable as you are, you've probably done something dumb when it comes to your retirement savings. Trust me, you're not alone.

Here are a few examples from the Moolala Community:

*"I deluded myself into thinking that doing something was doing enough. I put $50 a month into my RRSP for years but never increased the amount. I really don't know how I thought my retirement was going to turn out."*

—James, 45, contractor. Married with three kids.

*"I went through tough times in my marriage and we redirected all of our RRSP savings to counselling—a combined $750 a month. We ended up getting divorced and I never restarted any saving for retirement—for 11 years. I still managed to save a little for my kids' education but I stopped taking care of me."*

—Tara, 43, business analyst. Divorced with two kids.

*"I didn't start saving for retirement until I was 33. That was about ten years longer than I should have waited."*

—Karleen, 51, small business owner. Married.

*"I have allowed for too much 'dead money.' Why do I have so much tied up in money market funds? Probably because I haven't been good at setting aside time to properly research investments that will actually earn me money."*
> —Sunny, 42, academic. Single.

*"I had one of those Group RRSP plans from work and HR kept harassing me to sign some forms to participate. I never got around to it and only learned after I was laid off how much money I had flushed down the toilet."*
> —Cynthia, 50, journalist. Divorced with two adult children.

*"When I became self-employed, I stopped my RRSP monthly contribution and it was really hard to get caught up again."*
> —Beth, 50, project manager. Single.

*"I wish I had an interesting 'dumb thing.' Mine is such a boring 'dumb thing.' I haven't maxed out my RRSP in some years simply because of poor planning. Embarrassing."*
> —Shirley, 53, non-profit executive director. Widowed with two adult kids.

## The C Factors

Why do so many smart, capable people make such common mistakes? In my experience, it boils down to three factors: context, consequences, and complexity. Not surprisingly, I have named these the "C Factors."

1. **CONTEXT:** Smart people do dumb things with their retirement savings because they haven't created their own context for money. They haven't answered the question, "When it comes to retirement, what is my money for?" When you create a context for money that is relevant and empowering to you, doing smart things with your money becomes a heck of a lot easier.

2. **CONSEQUENCES:** Smart people sometimes live in denial about the consequences of their behaviour around money. Sure, there are a lot of demands on your money—student loans, groceries, a car, a mortgage, costs related to raising kids, and the occasional splurge that makes your life different from life in a convent or a cave. There are consequences to not saving for retirement, however, and addressing them will allow you to look at your situation more objectively, and help you adjust your behaviour so you get what you really want in life.

3. **COMPLEXITY:** Smart people often mismanage the level of complexity they need to have with their retirement savings. You might have too much complexity (following every move of the stock market in the hopes that you'll be able to time your buying and selling perfectly), or you might have too little (not understanding how your company's RRSP matching program works). Finding the right level of complexity for your circumstances and interests can go a long way towards lowering your stress and increasing your results.


## Conclusion

In Step 1 of the Moolala Method, we are going to start laying the foundation for your retirement savings by looking at each of the C Factors individually. You'll learn how to create your own context for your retirement savings, how to address the consequences of your behaviours around RRSPs that are not working for you, and how to find the optimal level of complexity for you and your situation, including a primer on RRSP basics. These strategies are the foundation you need to get a handle on your money so you can have the retirement you want.

# { 2 }

## CREATE YOUR OWN CONTEXT
### WHAT IS YOUR MONEY FOR?

---

**THE C FACTORS**

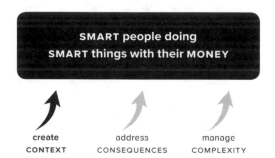

SMART people doing
SMART things with their MONEY

create
**CONTEXT**

address
CONSEQUENCES

manage
COMPLEXITY

CONTEXT IS the setting in which an event occurs. It is the back drop for everything you do with your money, and it can be either disempowering and discouraging or empowering and inspiring. Not surprisingly, the latter is much more productive in helping you get a handle on your money.

I first introduced the idea of "context" in *Moolala*. My assertion is that the failure to create an empowering and personal context for money is one of the key factors that causes smart people to do dumb things. Simply put, they haven't answered this question: "When it comes to retirement, what is my money for?"

Besides the obvious answer of food and shelter, a vehicle or bus pass, clothing and Netflix, when you think about your retirement, what is your money *for* in the broadest possible terms?

For some people, and you might be one of them, the first answer to the question "What is my money for?" is security. Money is for feeling confident that you can pay for basics, such as food and shelter. That's it. Full stop. There isn't anything else to it. But does that empower you? When you think about your retirement, does that excite you? Probably not. If your money is for "security," are you going to be willing to make the necessary effort to get a handle on it? Perhaps, but not likely.

I have seen a context that is empowering really make a difference. For example, think about the context for marriage. If you said to your soon-to-be spouse that "marriage is for security," you'd probably get a pillow thrown at you, or worse. Of course marriage *can* be for security. That's a part of it. But that isn't a particularly empowering context for most people. Another context might be that marriage is for love and companionship. Or passion. Or family. Contexts like these provide the foundation for those times when the marriage vows of "for better or for worse" get tested.

If you don't mind my getting all Oprah on you for a moment, *what I know for sure* is that the key to finding motivation for saving for retirement starts with creating *a context* for your money. For most of us, the statement "my money is for retirement" is about as inspiring as watching *Question Period* on TV. Unless you're 64 years old right now, it's unlikely that mantra will light a fire under you to start saving.

It took me many years to arrive at my own answer: *adventure*. When it comes to retirement, what is my money for?

My money is for adventure.

> What I know for sure is that the key to finding motivation for saving for retirement starts with creating a context for your money.

I plan on being in good health for a long time, and believe that my desire for a big adventurous life will still be strong 20, 30, even

40 years from now. I'm certain I am not going to wake up at the age of 65 and think, "Yup, bucket list complete! Now let's crack open the Sudoku and turn on C-Span for the latest on constitutional reform." I want to be able to afford adventure now *and* when my hair turns grey and I dress in Tilley from head to toe.

I see my life as one long (knock on wood) experience, not one that stops at some arbitrary age because I no longer go to an office five days a week. That word—adventure—helps motivate me to put some of my money into an RRSP on a regular basis.

So while "security" might be what your money is for today, now I'm going to ask you to look towards the future and get creative. Here are some examples from members of the Moolala Community. When it comes to retirement, my money is for:

*"Peace of mind."*

*"The grandchildren."*

*"Flexibility and fun."*

*"My family—to help my children and my grandchildren pursue their dreams in life."*

*"Experiences with family and friends."*

*"Travel. I want to retire young enough so I can see the world before my body or my mind goes. I'm not planning to leave anything behind."*

*"Enjoying life with my partner and daughter."*

*"Options. Giving me options."*

*"Prescription drugs and personal care. (I'm sure that the health care system will have collapsed by then.)"*

*"Experience and expression."*

*"Living life to the fullest."*

*"Supporting causes we believe in."*

*"Choices. I realized that if I didn't get my stuff together, I wouldn't have any choices when it came time to retire."*

*"Freedom: to enjoy retirement as we wish, and not necessarily living large… but without the incessant worry of money running out."*

---

**EXERCISE**    **Create a Context: When It Comes to Retirement, What Is Money For?**

As you saw above, people come up with an incredible range of answers to this question. Now is your opportunity to come up with an answer that's right for you.

**PONDER:** Take a blank sheet of paper and wander around your home. Look at your books, photos, mementoes. Look out your windows. As you do this, ponder these questions: What do you value? What do you enjoy? What is important to you in your life that money enables? What role do you want money to play in your life? How do you want to use it?

This question can be easy or hard, depending on your current mindset, life stage, and circumstances. You don't need to think about it too much, and this doesn't need to be *the* answer. In fact, the answer might evolve as the circumstances in your life evolve. Keep it simple, and aim for a word or two. This is the "big picture" answer of what money is for—we'll get into more specifics in the next exercise. If you find that you are struggling with this step, flip ahead a few pages for some ideas to help you answer the question.

When it comes to retirement, my money is for

_____.

## Retirement Is a Life Stage, Not an Activity

It is easy to forget that retirement is a life stage and not an activity. Life is made up of a series of stages—growing up, getting an education, starting a career, and perhaps getting married and having a family. Each of these stages has activities associated with it. Yet when the topic of retirement comes up, it sounds like an ephemeral, nebulous blob.

Let's blame the marketers, shall we? The volume of advertising around RRSP "season" makes Walmart's Christmas promotions look like a neighbourhood bake sale. But this cacophony doesn't ring true for most of us, so we tune it out.

### What do you actually want to *do* during your retirement?

Talk to anyone who is actually *in* the retirement stage of life and they will explain that you don't wake up in the morning and "do" retirement. You "do" things like golf, garden, read, hike, work part-time, hang out with the grandkids, and travel. And what you will "do" is different from what your parents, siblings, and friends "do," even though you'll all go through the same life stage. You don't need to have tee times in your calendar, but it does make a big difference to think about retirement in terms of what you will want to be "doing"—the activities that will fill your day.

I want to be doing things in New York City. This is the place where my husband, Dennis, and I plan on spending part of each year during retirement. When I think about what my retirement savings are for, they are for adventure, as I mentioned. And time in the Big Apple is a part of that. We'll organize a home exchange or rent a small apartment on the Upper West Side, ideally in a building with an elevator, because who knows how my knees will be working by then. We'll go see plays in grotty theatres downtown and get cheap tickets for Broadway. We'll walk the High Line urban park, have burgers at the Boat Basin overlooking the Hudson River, and read the Sunday edition of *The New York Times* over breakfast at our local diner.

We lived in New York for a number of years and love the energy and convenience of it. Almost everything is walkable and there is always something new to see and do. It is a great place to be a senior, aside from the outrageous cost of living. We know that the activities associated with this part of our adventure in retirement—flights, apartment, meals out—will be expensive, which is why we need to plan ahead.

## Why It Is Important to Determine What You Want

Determining what you want to do in retirement is basically a visioning exercise. You are creating a vision of what you want your life to look like in the future. It doesn't have to be a scripted, full-colour, 3D, Steven Spielberg-imagining of life. I know you're busy—a few simple ideas will work fine. But it is important to do this exercise for two reasons: first, because it makes retirement real, and second, because it will give you a sense of how much this vision is going to cost.

### Making retirement real

Retirement is not some glossy ad featuring smiling, grey-haired former super-models tooling around Tuscany in an antique roadster. It is a real life stage. And it is headed your way. We get more motivated by and engaged with things that are tangible to us. I remember that simply buying a copy of *Let's Go—Europe* transformed my first backpacking trip from being a theoretical event to something that was actually going to happen if, that is, I focused on saving up the money.

It is virtually impossible to get fired up about the task of making your RRSP contribution. But it *is* possible to get fired up about the idea of travelling the world the year you turn 70—a very specific activity you could undertake when you retire.

Besides, you will need to replace more than just your income when you retire. Your job provided many other important things that you may not value until they are gone: social interaction, challenge, intellectual stimulation, a sense of purpose, and, of course, a way to spend your time. Identifying activities you will do in retirement will help to ensure you get what you need to feel happy and fulfilled once your working days are done.

### Calculating the cost

The second reason having a sense of what you want to do in your retirement is important is because it will help you figure out what that retirement will cost. What *you* want isn't going to cost the same as what someone else wants. If your activities are cheap, you can save less of a nest egg; if your activities are expensive, then you'll need to save more. Playing "Angry Birds" (the 2034 version) with the grandkids is going to cost way less than travelling the world in search of real birds to watch.

Determining what you want to do *then* will help you figure out *how much* you're going to need to save *now*.

## But I'm Too Young To Be Thinking About This

You might be thinking, "I'm way, way too young to be thinking about this." I know exactly what you mean. Because I'm too young to be thinking about it too. Or you might be thinking, "Life is too short. I'm not going to wait until retirement to do the stuff I want." Of course you aren't going to wait and neither am I. Still, this is an important question to ponder, even though you're young and focused on living in the now.

My advice for the next exercise? Keep it simple. Spend only a few minutes on it. And remember that you can change your answer down the road. The point of this exercise is to get you thinking about what you want to do in your future so that you are more likely to do more smart things with your money now.

**Brainstorm Activities You Might Take On in Retirement**

**WRITE:** Take a moment to jot down a few ideas to answer this question: What activities do you want to take part in when you are no longer drawing a paycheque? Here are some examples from the Moolala Community to get the juices flowing.

- **TRAVEL:** Where do you want to go?

  *"Drink lots of good wine in the 'place where the grape was grown.'"*

  *"See every major tennis tournament in the world, starting with Wimbledon."*

  *"Go to my backyard. With a wee dram of Scotch."*

  *"Travel with our little trailer, finding mostly undiscovered fun spots to explore and enjoy."*

  *"Walk along beaches and in rainforests in Costa Rica."*

  *"Travel wherever the road takes us (in reliable and comfortable automobiles!)."*

- **EXPERIENCES:** What do you want to experience?

  *"Climb the seven summits."*

  *"Compete in the World Series of Poker."*

  *"Run a marathon on every continent."*

  *"Go on a roller coaster world tour."*

  *"Live in India for six months at a time and learn from my yoga teacher."*

*"No idea what I want, really. Except to have the freedom to do what I want at the drop of a hat. That is most appealing."*

- **HOME:** In what sort of place, or places, do you want to be living?

*"Live in my same house for as long as I'm healthy."*

*"Never spend more than two months in a row in winter."*

*"Downsize to a condo so I don't have to worry about maintenance."*

*"Buy a tiny little shack on the beach in Nicaragua and live there six months a year."*

*"Have two homes, one in each hemisphere."*

*"Have a condo in town but live in Italy for the better part of each year."*

*"Buy a cottage to enjoy summers with extended family."*

- **HOBBIES:** How do you want to spend your time?

*"Putter around the garage and get to all the projects I never had the time for when I was working full-time."*

*"Go see cultural things like theatre and ballet that I don't have time to attend now."*

*"Slow down. Honestly, I imagine a slow and simple pace of life. Maybe gardening."*

*"Go boating."*

*"Write more books."*

*"Host artist retreats on our land."*

- **FAMILY:** What do you want for your family life?

  *"Host an annual 'Grandma and Grandpa camp' for the grandkids."*

  *"Take my nephews on ski trips."*

  *"Support the higher education of our grandbabies and take them on fun adventures."*

  *"Spend our summers in Portugal with my partner's family."*

  *"Be able to travel with family members and future grandchildren."*

- **HEALTH:** What do you want for your health?

  *"Be present and healthy for every major family milestone."*

  *"Have access to private health care if needed for myself and family."*

  *"Do more yoga. And slow down and just enjoy the view."*

  *"Be able to afford a personal support worker to keep me in my own home."*

- **CONTRIBUTION:** Where do you want to make a difference in the community?

  *"Contribute my art to reach as many people as need it, all over the world."*

  *"Mentor troubled youth."*

  *"Support charity work in the area of women's health."*

  *"Establish a family foundation."*

  *"Volunteer at my church."*

  *"Do something charitable in every country I visit—build a home, teach a course, finance a small business, leave behind school books."*

- **WORK:** What sorts of jobs will you do?

  *"Continue my consulting, but only with people I like on projects I love."*

  *"Do some meaningful paid work well into my 70s and even 80s."*

  *"Get a job at Home Depot. I hang out there enough as it is!"*

You might not have ideas for activities in every area—and don't worry if all your ideas change completely in a month or a decade. The point is that you've started thinking about retirement in a real and tangible way. And when something is tangible, it is way easier to plan for it.

| AREA | ACTIVITIES |
|---|---|
| Travel | |
| Experiences | |
| Home | |
| Hobbies | |
| Family | |
| Health | |
| Contribution | |
| Work | |

**TALK:** If you are in a relationship, have this conversation about retirement with your spouse. Recognize that some of your answers may be similar and others may be different. Or talk about your answers with a good friend—it will make a big difference to hear your answers out loud and will likely provide some perspective on what you want to do (and absolutely do *not* want to do). Don't get hung up on having the "perfect" answer—retirement is still years away, after all. And if you simply don't have a clue, think about someone you know who is retired and rip off his or her activities. That will suffice for now.

## Conclusion

The first "C Factor" that prevents smart, capable people from doing smart things with their retirement savings is not having a context for it. Creating a context that is tangible, empowering, personal, and consistent with your values is critical to getting a handle on your money so you can live the life you want. Now we are going to look at some important things you do with your money that you might need to rein in. These areas will become increasingly clear as we turn to address the second C Factor: the consequences of your behaviour around money.

# { 3 }

## ADDRESS THE CONSEQUENCES
### RRSPS MAY NOT BE COOL, BUT
### NEITHER IS SPONGING OFF YOUR KIDS

---

**THE C FACTORS**

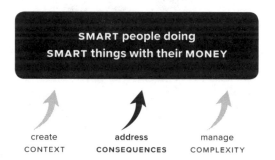

SMART people doing
SMART things with their MONEY

| create | address | manage |
| CONTEXT | CONSEQUENCES | COMPLEXITY |

T HE SECOND C FACTOR is consequences: smart people do dumb things with their money because they are unaware of the consequences of their behaviour.

Most of us have behaviours around money that we would call strengths, which have positive consequences. And then we have behaviours that we would call weaknesses, which have negative consequences. Given that the purpose here is to get a better handle on our money, we're going to focus on those behaviours that you would say are weaknesses.

For many years my big weakness was a lack of knowledge. Despite receiving an honours business degree from a great university, I didn't understand the most basic things about investing. My naïveté lead me to take way more risk than I should have, placing some of my hard-earned retirement savings in some complicated financial product that ended up losing half its value within a year. If knowledge is power, I didn't have enough to power a night-light. And that cost me a good chunk of change.

In all likelihood you have weaknesses too. Now that you have a sense of what sort of a retirement you want, it's helpful to look at some common weaknesses around money and the consequences associated with them. Note that I said "helpful," but I did not say "fun." This section of the guide can be challenging because most of us prefer to bury our heads in the sand and stay oblivious to how we might be mismanaging our money. But I promise you that it will be worth both your time and your emotional energy. And you have my full permission to reward yourself with chocolate or the beverage of your choice upon completion.

Addressing the consequences of your behaviour around money will allow you to have more of what you really want in life: more freedom, more choices, more experiences, more of whatever it is you've decided your money is for. In my case, I'm willing to examine the consequences of my behaviour around money because of *adventure*. The better I am at addressing them, the more adventure I will have in my life.

So, what's in it for you?

Looking at the consequences of my behaviour around money will allow me to have:

[Insert your Moolala Context from chapter 2 here.]

---

## Retirement Savings Behaviours: The Weaknesses

The retirement savings behaviours that you call weaknesses will be unique to you—so will the consequences. But there certainly are some clear themes, as you can see in these examples from the Moolala Community.

**KNOWLEDGE:** Being unaware of what you need to save or how to invest in a way that will get you what you want.

*"I have absolutely no interest in personal finance, and neither does my wife. But that means that we are totally clueless about retirement savings and we certainly don't have a plan we feel good about. Most of our friends are in the same boat, but that doesn't seem to make us feel better anymore. We get really stressed out during RRSP season."*
   —Kamal, 41, policy analyst. Married.

*"I depend on my advisor to tell me where to put my money. I'm not interested in educating myself on the best options for investing, and I tend to make decisions based on gut versus information. But I have seen in a few instances how much that has cost me and I don't like it."*
   —Vivian, 36, sales rep. Single.

**SPENDING:** Putting money towards things other than retirement savings.

*"We love our house. It has everything we ever wanted, but that comes at a big price. Now that we've moved in we realize that we can't contribute what we would like towards our RRSPs. And if interest rates go up we won't be able to contribute much at all. I feel kind of helpless about it."*
   —Jonathon, 52, designer. Married with two kids.

*"My marriage is stressful and my job is a drag. I feel like a doll that has been broken. And in the absence of anyone coming to fix me up, I spend money. I feel like I deserve to spend money. Not wild amounts, but more than we can afford. I know it doesn't fix my mental state, and probably makes it worse. But in the moment it provides comfort."*
   —Olivia, 47, benefits administrator. Married with three kids.

**EARNING:** Not focusing enough on bringing money in.

*"I have been insufficiently concerned with realizing my earning potential. I have sacrificed pay for satisfaction, which everyone I know says, in theory, one should do. But I'm now 42 and in my peak earning years and I am simply not earning enough to realize all of my spending desires. I need to make a shift."*
  —Andrew, 42, academic. Single.

*"I stayed home when the kids were young. Now that they are in school full-time I know I should go back to work because God knows we need the money. But my self-confidence is low and I never really loved the work I did. And, frankly, our family life is much easier because I can run all the errands during the day."*
  —Cathy, 37, payroll accountant. Married with two kids.

**SAVING:** Simply not saving enough.

*"My weakness is that I save only randomly and then hope it will all work out by the time I actually retire. It is basically the 'cross your fingers and make a wish' retirement strategy versus having a plan. The paltry amount I have saved reflects this very well."*
  —Diane, 50, consultant. Married.

*"Saving is a serious weakness for me. Taking money out of savings to use towards today's lifestyle has been my downfall. I know I won't have the income to support the lifestyle I want to have when I retire. This creates stress and anxiety for me."*
  —Sean, 33, small business owner. Single.

**INVESTING:** Failing to put your money to work for you.

*"I haven't found a way to think about investing that feels interesting and engaging. I have a self-limiting belief that I'm not good with numbers. I feel dumb and not on top of my money, which is a pretty big consequence now that I think about it."*
  —Noah, 48, academic administrator. Married with two kids.

*"I just can't seem to get my head around how to invest money. I have $75,000 sitting with an advisor, who now wants to charge a $250 fee just to keep it. I know I need to move it, but I'm still very stuck around this. This is really frustrating because I know how wasteful it is to have the money just sitting in cash."*
    —Marcus, 35, pharmacist. Single

**ORGANIZATION:** Not having a basic retirement savings plan or staying on top of what you need to do and when you need to do it.

*"I am so busy living my life in a 'moment to moment' way I am not giving my future enough thought. I want someone to just tell me what to do and I'll do it. I am disorganized when it comes to money and I know that is hurting me financially."*
    —Christie, 42, designer. Married.

*"This is really embarrassing—I actually made the RRSP contributions and then didn't file my income taxes and use the deduction."*
    —Poonum, 38, account executive. Single.

**COMMUNICATION:** Not having an open dialogue with your family and/or your financial advisor about what you want for retirement and the plan to get it.

*"Retirement planning doesn't interest either of us, so we're very, very passive about it all. In fact, when I see my financial advisor's number on call display, I let it ring through to voice mail. I just can't bear to talk to him."*
    —Jonathon, 52, designer. Married with two kids.

*"My husband and I have very different views about saving for retirement and we have a very hard time talking about it without arguing. So we basically avoid the topic entirely."*
    —Beatrice, 37, writer. Married with one child.

**TAKING ACTION:** Not doing what you need to do in order to get what you want.

*"I am getting better. I have fewer investment products and lower fees. But my weakness is not dumping the dogs and moving my money to something that might actually grow over time."*
  —Roula, 32, teacher. Married with one child on the way.

*"I lack any sense of urgency when it comes to contributing to my RRSPs. I keep saying I'll put money aside next year, and each year passes and I don't invest. I know I'm losing big money that I could have earned in interest, and I feel I'm falling further behind."*
  —Steve, 55, corporate trainer. Married with two adult children.

## Tangible and Intangible Consequences

The consequences of your retirement savings behaviours come in two forms: tangible and intangible. Tangible consequences are easy to identify and measure, such as not having enough money to retire when and how you want to, missing out on compound interest, paying excess income tax, wasting time by procrastinating, or failing to work effectively with your spouse or financial advisor on the plan. Intangible consequences are tougher to identify, impossible to measure, and often related to how you feel about yourself, your family, and your life. Intangible consequences include stress, anxiety, anger, disappointment, stupidity, frustration, conflict, or regret.

While working with the Moolala Community I've found that most people can identify their weaknesses easily. What they find much more difficult is drawing the link between the weaknesses and the consequences. It is a blind spot for most people and a particularly important blind spot to reveal because if you can't see the consequences of your behaviour, why on earth would you bother changing it?

| EXERCISE | **Identify the Consequences of Your Behaviour Around Retirement Savings** |
|---|---|

As I mentioned, the consequences of your behaviour around retirement savings are unique to you. Let's take a closer look.

**BRAINSTORM:** Think about some of the behaviours that you have around money that you would say are weaknesses. Consider areas such as knowledge, spending, earning, saving, investing, organization, communication, and taking action. Then, for each of these behaviours, write down in a table some of the tangible and intangible consequences that relate to those behaviours. (A worksheet is available on moolala.ca.)

Here's an example:

| BEHAVIOUR | TANGIBLE CONSEQUENCES | INTANGIBLE CONSEQUENCES |
|---|---|---|
| Neglecting my savings | I won't be able to retire at age 65, which I really want to do | • Stress<br>• Frustration |

| BEHAVIOUR | TANGIBLE CONSEQUENCES | INTANGIBLE CONSEQUENCES |
|---|---|---|
|  |  |  |
|  |  |  |
|  |  |  |
|  |  |  |

**PRIORITIZE:** Circle the three behaviours that are the most significant for you, based on the severity of the consequences associated with them. This will give you a sense of what to focus on first.

**FORGIVE:** Whatever has happened has already happened. That milk has been spilled and feeling guilty about it isn't helpful. So take a moment right now to look in a mirror and say to yourself, "I forgive you." Simplistic? Yes. Easy? No. Helpful? Absolutely. Forgiveness is a part of addressing the consequences of your behaviour and moving on.

Now, congratulate yourself on developing a bit of self-knowledge about your financial behaviour. We'll be coming up with ways to improve those behaviours and address those consequences throughout this guide, so keep this list handy.

## The Power of Compound Interest

There are many temptations that can push RRSP contributions to the bottom of your priority list. When those temptations start to overwhelm you, here are two little words that may help you make a more thoughtful choice: Compound. Interest.

Uh-oh, did your eyes just glaze over? How about this: Compound (Brad-Pitt!) interest. Compound (Angelina-Jolie!) interest. Is that better? Compound Interest—that is, earning interest on your interest—means you make significantly more money over a period of time without having to do a damn thing but contribute regularly to your savings. Simply put, if you don't start now, you'll miss out on a whole lot of "free" money.

In the example below, the early bird saves $100 a month for forty years and the late bloomer saves $200 a month for twenty years. Assuming their money grows at the rate of 7% per year, even though they both contribute the same amount, $48,000, the early bird's total savings will be $264,000 compared to the late bloomer's $105,000. That is a *massive* difference, and it is all a result of the interest paid on the interest. That's the power of compounding: the early bird's money had twice as much time to grow.

## Compound Interest

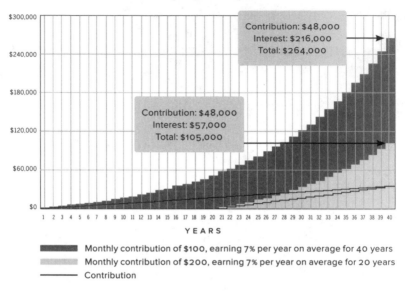

Sure, there are lots of reasons why it is hard to start to invest when we're younger. But as you can see, the consequences of starting late are significant. It really all boils down to making trade-offs among competing demands for your money.

### Making trade-offs to support your retirement

Life is a series of trade-offs. If you think about it, every day you are trading off time, energy, and money. For example, the more sweet treats I eat—and I do love my sweet treats—the more I need to exercise to prevent my weight from ballooning out of control. The more time I spend working, the less time I have for dance parties with my daughter, Abby.

I don't like making trade-offs, and I don't imagine you do either. But saving for retirement does mean making trade-offs. Unless you have abundant disposable income, you will have to trade off money that you'd really like to spend now for future savings to ensure that you have enough for your needs and wants in retirement. Eating out, buying shoes, and taking great vacations gives you pleasure in the now, and it is a trade-off against pleasure, or even sustenance, in the future.

Yet most people don't see the trade-offs they are making with their retirement savings. They don't appreciate the tangible and intangible consequences of their behaviour.

You are no longer one of those people. You are now waking up to the consequences of your behaviour around retirement savings, and you'll get better at identifying the trade-offs you're making as you make them. Here is an example from the Moolala Community:

> **Life is a series of trade-offs. If you think about it, every day you are trading off time, energy, and money.**

*"Instead of contributing to my RRSP I am spending my money on eating out and buying books, both of which I love. I commit to trimming the amount I spend at restaurants and using the library instead of building one of my own."*
—Lynne, 41, entrepreneur. Married with two kids.

## Conclusion

The second C Factor that prevents smart, capable people from doing smart things with their retirement savings is not addressing the consequences of their behaviour. In this chapter, you identified the behaviours we could call weaknesses, and you've forgiven yourself for those behaviours. Now it's time to move on so you can get more of what you really want in retirement. Fortunately, addressing the consequences is easier than you might think, especially if you don't make things too complex.

# { 4 }

## MANAGE COMPLEXITY
### FOCUS ON THE BASICS

---

**THE C FACTORS**

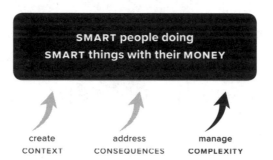

COMPLEXITY REFERS to something that is composed of many interconnected parts. Certainly your retirement savings fit that definition. Smart people often mismanage the level of complexity they need to have with their RRSPs. Some people have *too much* complexity when it comes to their money—too many investments or accounts that they either don't understand or have a tough time keeping on top of. Or they have *too little* complexity—for example, not knowing what an RRSP is or how much money they will need to retire.

Finding the right level of complexity for your circumstances and interests can go a long way towards lowering your stress level and increasing your results. But for many smart people, their fundamental disinterest, plus a few buckets of RRSP jargon, make it really hard to figure out what the right level is. Here are some examples from the Moolala Community of how you can have too much or too little complexity in your retirement savings.

### Too much complexity

*"I have my money scattered in 100 different funds. If I kick off before getting my act together, no one is ever going to find it all."*

*"I spend a lot of time figuring out how to split my savings between RRSPs and TFSAs. I always end up exhausted and confused."*

*"I track the stock market obsessively and second guess my investment guy."*

### Too little complexity

*"I bought RRSPs over my mobile phone this year… on the deadline day. I don't know what the hell I bought. I just hoped for the best."*

*"Every year my financial advisor calls me up and tells me to send him RRSP money. I do. And that is it."*

*"My HR person has tried to make me read the pamphlet about my Group RRSP thingy. But I just can't do it. I know I should. I just can't seem to get through it."*

Getting a handle on your retirement savings doesn't need to be complicated. Finding the right level of complexity for your finances is about gaining some basic knowledge, learning a few simple skills, and developing some good habits that will help you stay engaged over the long term. Let's start by building up your knowledge of RRSPS…

## Gain the Basic Knowledge
## The Who, What, When, Where, Why and How of RRSPs

Here is a relatively "low complexity" review of the basics of RRSPs, which we'll be building on in the rest of the guide: the who, what, when, where, why, and how—though not in the boring old conventional order.

### WHAT IS AN RRSP?
### An account with tax benefits

A "Registered Retirement Savings Plan," or RRSP, is a type of account that allows you to shelter some of your income from the tax people, so it can grow into a nice nest egg to fund your retirement.

I think of an RRSP as a wine cellar for your retirement savings. A wine cellar is a place for you to store your Pinot Noir. It protects it from the summer heat and allows it to age into a mature, more flavourful and more valuable wine. An RRSP is a place for you to store some of your money. It protects that money from income tax, allowing your nest egg to become more valuable over time.

> I think of an RRSP as a wine cellar for your retirement savings

A wine cellar *holds* wine, but you can't drink a wine cellar itself. An RRSP *holds* investments—such as mutual funds, exchange-traded funds, stocks, or bonds—but it isn't an investment in itself. You can choose super safe or riskier investments to put in your RRSP, depending on your risk tolerance and circumstances.

### Bulking up your tax refund

The reason an RRSP is so compelling financially is that you defer income tax on the money you put into it. Your RRSP contribution allows you to claim a tax deduction, which decreases your taxable income and increases your tax refund. So when you put $5,000 into your RRSP, it reduces your taxable income by $5,000. Hooray! If you were in a 30% tax bracket, you would have paid about $1,500 in income tax on that money. But because it is safely stored in your RRSP you don't have to pay that tax, resulting in a $1,500 refund cheque. And the $5,000 can grow inside your RRSP, shielded from tax, for years and years. Then, when you're retired, you'll be able to withdraw the money from your RRSP to pay your bills. And while you will pay tax on the money then, that tax will likely be charged at a lower rate than when you first earned the money, because your income during your retirement will be lower than during your working years and you will likely be in a lower tax bracket.

### WHY ARE RRSPS A GOOD THING?
### The benefits of tax deduction, tax-deferred compounding, and flexibility

There are three enormous benefits of putting money into this metaphorical wine cellar, instead of just parking it in a regular savings account: the tax deduction, of course, the elaborately named benefit of tax-deferred compounding, and flexibility.

### Tax deduction: Reducing your tax bill now

Income contributed to an RRSP gives you a tax deduction that reduces your income tax bill immediately. This contribution allows you to defer the tax you'll need to pay on that income until your retirement when you'll likely be in a lower tax bracket. Whether you earn great gobs of money or little dollops of money from your job, you will be taxed on the whole amount—*except* for the one special amount you are allowed to put into your RRSP wine cellar, where the government can't get at it for a long, long time.

Let's say you make $50,000 per year and contribute $5,000 into your RRSP every year. You are able to deduct this amount, bringing your taxable income down to $45,000. This allows you to defer $1,500 in income tax every year.

**RRSP contributions reduce your taxable income**

|  | $0 RRSP CONTRIBUTION | $5,000 RRSP CONTRIBUTION |
|---|---|---|
| Taxable income | $50,000 | $45,000 |
| Tax rate* | 30% | 30% |
| Combined federal and provincial tax bill | $15,000 | $13,500 |
| Deferred Tax | $0 | **$1,500** |

\*   Note: Your actual tax rate depends on factors such as type of income and province of residence. The 30% figure is for illustration purposes only. For more on tax rates, visit moolala.ca

In very tangible terms, the tax deduction often means that you'll get a juicy tax refund every spring—a refund that you would not have received had you not contributed to your RRSP.

It is important to make the most of the RRSP tax incentive by saving money for your retirement yourself because the income you'll receive from government sources is not likely to be enough to live on after you stop working. We'll look at this more closely in chapter 5.

**Tax-deferred compounding: Savings on steroids**

The second benefit of an RRSP is that your money will be able to grow in value—just like your wine—tax-deferred. If your money were held outside of your RRSP, in a non-registered investment account or even a boring old savings account, for example, you would pay tax on the interest income as soon was it is earned. But inside an RRSP it is sheltered from tax until you withdraw it, allowing you to make the most of the magic of compound interest. Let's take a look at how that tax-deferred growth can put your savings on steroids.

**Investing in a savings account versus an RRSP**

|  | SAVINGS ACCOUNT | RRSP |
|---|---|---|
| Amount invested annually | $5,000 | $5,000 |
| Years invested | 30 years | 30 years |
| Tax rate | 30% | N/A |
| Average annual return | 5% | 5% |
| Total savings | $267,000 | $349,000 |
| Difference in total savings |  | **$82,000** |

This table shows that $5,000 invested annually would grow to $349,000 inside an RRSP—that is $82,000 more than if the same amount had been held in a savings account. The reason the difference is so large is because the money was able to earn interest on its interest without being taxed each year. If you'd like to try this with some numbers of your own, go to moolala.ca and follow one of the links we've provided there.

Once you retire and start taking cash out of your RRSP you will, of course, have to pay tax on it. Did you really think the Canadian government would simply forget about lil' ol' you and your wine cellar full of money? But you will have benefited immensely by that time, having essentially deferred paying a debt without being penalized, which is a rare and wonderful thing in this world.

**Flexibility: Making your money work for you**
The third benefit of an RRSP is that it allows some flexibility with your finances. For example, you can contribute money to something called a spousal RRSP, which will allow you to split income with your beloved. I'll discuss this more in chapter 8. You may also have the flexibility to borrow from your RRSP under the Home Buyers' Plan or the Lifelong Learning Plan to buy your first home or to fund your education. (I'll discuss these in more detail in Appendix

A.) So, if you are hesitant to contribute to an RRSP because you want to save the money for a down payment on your first house or go back to school, you might be able to have your wine and drink it too.

~~~~~~~~~~~~~~~~~~~~~~~~~~~~~~~~~~~~~~~~~~~~~~~~

 ## Interest Rates Are Crazy Low.
## Is an RRSP *Really* the Best Way to Save?

### QUESTION:

*"I'm really concerned about contributing to an RRSP because of low interest rates. Is it really the best way to save for retirement? I feel it's just another way for the government to control our spending and still tax the death out of us. Please ... I'm serious about my concerns."*

### ANSWER:

Yes. RRSPs really are the best way to save for retirement. That is, for those of us who don't have a pension plan that will cover our needs and wants after we leave the workforce.

There are other options, of course. You could invest in rental properties and use the income they spin off to pay for the wild excesses of your dotage. Or you could start a business and pay yourself dividends instead of saving inside an RRSP.

These are options, but they require an elusive combination of capital, hard work, and luck. For most of us, the RRSP is still the best way to save for retirement because it allows us to defer taxes into the future, when we will presumably be earning less and therefore required to pay less tax.

### An RRSP is just a container for your investments

Remember, an RRSP is not an investment in and of itself. It is a container for investments, like a knapsack for your lunch or a wine cellar for your wine. You can't actually invest in an RRSP itself, but you can invest in things like mutual funds, stocks or bonds that go into an RRSP.

So when interest rates are low, they affect only the performance of any fixed income investments (such as GICs, bonds, or bond funds) you may hold in your RRSP, not the RRSP itself. If you are really concerned about low interest rates, you could invest entirely in stocks, which have historically performed better over long periods of time, but with more ups and downs. We'll be taking a closer look at what you can put into your RRSP and in what proportions in chapter 12.

### The government can't control our spending

The government can't control our spending. Look no further than our horrifying debt to income ratio of 150%, which means that for every $1,000 in after-tax income, Canadians owe $1,500. Wowsa. If the government could control our spending, I'm sure they would, if only to minimize the risks associated with so many of its citizens carrying so much debt. Think about it—if you have a lot of debt and lose your job you won't be able to pay your bills. This could put a lot of pressure on social programs and creditors, which is not good for the economy.

The government can't control our spending, but they certainly can influence it either by layering on taxes to discourage certain behaviours or offering tax breaks to encourage others. Take smoking, for example. Huge taxes on cigarettes have helped to reduce the number of smokers lighting up in this country. By the same logic, by offering tax incentives for RRSP contributions, the government hopes to encourage Canadians to save for their retirement. The statisticians in Ottawa know that our social safety net just isn't large enough or strong enough to hold up every 75-year-old from Comox to Cape Breton. People need to save on their own for retirements and the RRSP is one way to encourage them to do so.

### Death and taxes: Taxed to death

You're feisty about the level of taxes we pay in this country. I get it. They are higher than we taxpayers want, but lower than in most other developed countries in the world. (The Organisation for Economic Co-operation and Development ranked Canada's tax burden as twenty-fifth of the thirty-four OECD member countries. Belgium was first, followed by Germany.) But again, if you hate paying taxes, that is a point in favour of the RRSP. It is one of the very few tax breaks our government offers us—the ability to defer taxes to the future.

### Retirement savings: Time to get to it

My hunch is that you would have preferred a different answer to your question: one that offered up a new, different, and less onerous option than saving in an RRSP. Or perhaps you were looking for a diatribe against government or taxes or aging—anything that would take the responsibility for saving for retirement off your shoulders. I got nothin'. Sorry. But what I do got is a simple plan to help you get momentum on retirement savings. Just stay with me.

~~~~~~~~~~~~~~~~~~~~~~~~~~~~~~~~~~~~~~~~~~

#### HOW MUCH CAN YOU CONTRIBUTE TO YOUR RRSP?
**Your contribution room with a view**

The amount you can contribute to your RRSP is based on a percentage of your prior year's earned income, up to a maximum amount. As of 2014, the current percentage is 18% and the maximum amount is around $24,000—it goes up a little bit each year. If you are one of those lucky people with a pension from your employer, a pension adjustment will reduce your RRSP contribution room. If you contribute under your limit in a given year, you can carry over your unused "contribution room" into future years.

Here's an example: let's say you earned $70,000 last year. You would be allowed to contribute 18% of that, or $12,600, to your RRSP this year. However, if you were only able to find $5,000 to contribute to your RRSP, you would have $7,600 in unused contribution room to carry over to the future.

Now, I know that, like most people, you have many competing demands on your disposable income, so it might seem like an acid-fuelled delusion to think that you'll ever get close to contributing that 18% figure. The fact is that very few people actually max out their contribution room, but I promise that if you continue to work through the *Moolala Guide to Rockin' Your RRSP* you'll find some ways to contribute more than you do today. We'll look at such topics as contribution room, over-contributions, and "top-up" loans in more detail in chapter 9. In the meantime, go to the Canada Revenue Agency (CRA) website or moolala.ca for more information on your RRSP contribution limit.

### WHERE CAN YOU OPEN UP AN RRSP ACCOUNT?
**As easy to open as a regular bank account**

You can set up an RRSP at most financial institutions, including banks, credit unions, discount brokers, full-service brokers, or mutual fund companies. They all offer "wine cellars" of different kinds. Some RRSPs are designed to hold only certain types of investments—for example, mutual funds—and others can hold almost any type of investment. We'll talk about that more in chapter 12. You may also open up your RRSP through your employer, in the form of a Group RRSP. That topic is coming up in chapter 8.

### HOW DO YOU MAKE AN RRSP CONTRIBUTION?
**As simple as banking online**

We will cover all the mechanics of RRSPs in chapter 8, but here is the super simple answer. You open up an account and then transfer money into it either at a branch or online. Then you'll receive a form to include with your income tax return that will reduce the amount of tax you have to pay. In most cases, this means that you will receive a tax refund—and a much larger tax refund than you would have received had you not contributed to your RRSP.

### WHEN IS THE DEADLINE?
**You must have noticed the advertising at the end of February**

The deadline for making a contribution to your RRSP for the previous tax year is sixty days after January 1. That usually means the deadline is March 1, except in a leap year or when that date falls on a Sunday. Unless you are hibernating along with the bears, you'll see, hear, and feel the loud and constant reminders from the financial industry through January and February.

Canada is filled with people who cut close to the deadline, either because they are thrill-seekers who like the adrenalin rush, or because they are chronic procrastinators who never met a deadline they didn't resist. I have been known to curse the gods while waiting in a long line at the bank, but that isn't necessary if you stay engaged during the year. We'll talk more about how to do that in chapters 13 and 14, including a super simple way to automate your RRSP contributions.

### WHO CAN CONTRIBUTE TO AN RRSP?
**If you have income, you're in**

If you have "earned income" you are eligible to open an RRSP, up until the year you turn 71. In this case "earned" means that the income came from a salary versus from a rental property or a dividend, for example.

Anyone with earned income can contribute—even young people who are just starting out in part-time jobs. But there are some situations in which RRSPs aren't the best option for retirement savings. We'll cover this question in chapter 8.

## Conclusion

The third C Factor that prevents smart, capable people from doing smart things with their retirement savings is not having the right level of complexity for their circumstances and interests. You might have either too much complexity or too little. Finding the right level of complexity for you and your finances begins with gaining some basic knowledge about RRSPs. In Step 1 of the Moolala Method, you did a lot of great work to lay the foundation of your knowledge about RRSPs. Now, in Step 2, we'll build on that knowledge by determining how much you'll need to save to ensure you get the retirement you want.

# STEP 2

---

# DETERMINE HOW MUCH YOU NEED

---

# { 5 }

## THE NEST EGG

### CALCULATE HOW
### MUCH IS ENOUGH

---

"**I**T'S JUST a flesh wound."

This is the key line from a great scene in the movie *Monty Python and the Holy Grail*. King Arthur and the Black Knight confront each other in a forest and very quickly a sword fight erupts. King Arthur soon chops off both of the Black Knight's arms. Still, he keeps fighting, as fake blood spurts from the stumps.

> KING ARTHUR. Look, you stupid bastard. You've got no arms left.
> BLACK KNIGHT. Yes I have.
> KING ARTHUR. Look!
> BLACK KNIGHT. It's just a flesh wound.

The Black Knight is either a deluded optimist or a dope, depending on your point of view. Oblivious to the injuries he has suffered, he pretends everything is just fine and that's what makes it so funny.

Unfortunately, most Canadians are equally oblivious to their retirement savings, which is not quite so funny.

Few retirement-related topics provoke as much emotion as talking about "how much is enough?" I asked members of the Moolala Community how they felt when they thought about the topic. Here are some of their answers:

*"I'm terrified to find out. I don't want to know. I would just rather not know."*

*"I have no idea. I think my wife has figured this out. She is the family CFO."*

*"I am terrified—I am confident it is a number that can never be attained."*

*"I'm scared. I don't think I will ever be able to retire unless I inherit or someone takes care of me—as I'm not married and don't have kids."*

*"What's one level up from petrified?"*

*"I feel anxious and nervous because I don't know how much is enough."*

*"I feel resigned to my fate. It doesn't matter how much is enough because I can only work with the money I have available."*

*"I feel panicky."*

*"I am a bit terrified to find out. But I have limited emotional and mental space/energy to think about it right now—really need to get my debt under control."*

*"I'm overwhelmed because I bet the number is going to be big."*

*"I feel Zen. It'll never be enough, but it's more than enough."*

*"I'm just trying to save as much as I can, create as much wealth as I can, and defer as much as I can."*

*"I feel I need to take action."*

*"I feel a sense of creeping uncertainty (even if the uncertainty is not rational)."*

Given all these emotions, perhaps it is no surprise that so few people have any idea of what size their nest egg will need to be. And if you don't know how much you need you can't possibly develop a plan to get it. What I've found to be true is that knowing the number and developing a plan to achieve it goes a long way toward alleviating negative feelings. Why? Because it gives you a measure of control over your financial future.

I think of the RRSP as a wine cellar, as I mentioned earlier. You're saving money now for some good times in the future and so you need to make sure that your wine cellar is well stocked to last you for the duration of your retirement.

But how much is enough? The answer to that critical question is a function of a number of things—what other income you have, how much income you are going to need to fund your life in retirement, how long the money needs to last, and how well your investments perform. Let's go into each of those factors in a bit more detail.

## Back to the Future: Where Your Retirement Income Comes From

For most of us, a large part of our retirement income is likely to come from the nest egg we have built up during our working years. Assuming you don't have a trust fund, you and/or your spouse probably do some sort of work that brings in an income. It could be a salary from a company, commission from sales you make, tips from grateful customers, fees from freelance projects or profit from your own business. Wherever it comes from, money that is somehow connected to the energy you put in at work arrives in your bank account.

After you retire, you will no longer be receiving income from your work. You'll receive some money every month from the government in the form of Old Age Security (OAS) and likely the Canada Pension Plan (CPP), and some of you will have pension income from your former employer. But most of us won't have a full pension and would find it very hard to live on just the payments from OAS and CPP. (To find out how much money you can expect from OAS and

CPP, refer to the sidebar below. The average amount is about $1000 per month.) So we will need to squirrel away a big enough nest egg to put food on the table and give us the financial freedom to take part in some of the activities we'd like to do once we become the king or queen of our calendars again.

Your nest egg will provide income in two ways. First, there will be some sort of investment return on your money. Say you have $500,000 invested in bonds that earn 3% per year in interest, for an annual interest payment of $15,000. You can take that $15,000 and use it for food, flights, or foliage. And since you haven't touched the principal, your bonds will earn another $15,000 in interest the next year.

Second, you can use some of your nest egg's principal to pay your bills. Of course, the more of that principal you spend, the less interest income you'll receive in the future and the faster your nest egg will deplete.

## What Can You Expect from OAS and CPP When You Retire?

Canada's Old Age Security program is a vital source of income for many retirees—some more than others, depending on what other earnings they've got coming their way. Simply put, the OAS goes to everyone over 65 who has lived in Canada for ten years or longer. The exact amount you'll receive varies somewhat based on how long you've lived in Canada and whether you qualify for a special allowance reserved for low-income retirees called the Guaranteed Income Supplement. The maximum monthly OAS benefit paid in January 2013 was $546.07. The amount is indexed to inflation, meaning that your monthly payment should increase alongside the price of a cup of coffee. However, if you bring in more than $70,000 a year in retirement, you are considered a high-income earner and part of your OAS payment will be "clawed back." You lose the entire amount if your net income in any year is about $115,000. It is also worth noting that as of 2023, the age of eligibility for OAS will gradually increase from 65 to 67 years old. So if you were born in 1958 or later, you will be affected by this change.

The Canadian Pension Plan also provides income to retirees, but only to those who have contributed to it. Depending on how much you contributed and for how long, your CPP payment could make up a slightly juicier piece of your retirement pie each month than what you'll receive from OAS. If, for instance, you have lived and worked in Canada for most of your adult life and earned an annual salary of approximately $40,000, at age 65 you will receive a CPP retirement pension of around $800 a month. That being said, the average CPP payout is about $600.

A super simple rule of thumb is that you'll receive about $1,000 per month or $12,000 per year from OAS and CPP combined. This number could swing a few hundred dollars per month in either direction based on your income and how much gets clawed back. If you want a more accurate number and not simply a rule of thumb, visit servicecanada.gc.ca to find out what you can expect from CPP and OAS based on your individual circumstances.

## What's Your Number?
## Figuring Out How Much Income You Need

The size of the nest egg you need to save will depend on how much income you will need in retirement. The basic rule of thumb is that you will need somewhere between 50% and 100% of the salary you earned, before tax, in your last year of full-time work to sustain your life without a paycheque. The percentage you choose has an enormous impact on the size of the nest egg you will require. If you choose 50%, it will be much easier to achieve your target nest egg than if you choose 100%. But will 50% of your pre-retirement income be enough?

I know what you're thinking: "But Bruce, I'm still in the early stages of my career. How can I possibly predict what sort of job I'll be doing, let alone how much I'll be earning or what percentage I'll need in thirty or forty years?" Great question. I talk it about in the section on "target retirement income" later in this chapter.

Before I do, let me provide my two cents on the debate around what percentage to use as a rule of thumb. There is a lot of discussion about what number will reflect your circumstances. Bill Morneau and Fred Vettese are the co-authors of the book *The Real Retirement: Why You Could Be Better Off Than You Think, and How to Make That Happen.* They argue that using just 50% could be more than enough, and they believe that the financial services industry is using too high a rule of thumb for most Canadians. Other critics point out that using gross income versus net income can be misleading because your tax situation can be much different in retirement than when you're working.

I don't mean to sound flippant, but I'm more interested in you having a number than having the most precise number possible. My rationale is simple: so few people have any clue what sort of nest egg they need for retirement that my first priority is to see you arrive at a ballpark figure. Once you have a ballpark figure, and as you get closer to retirement, you can refine your estimate of how much income you'll need. You would do that by taking your current net income and subtracting out savings, because when you are in retirement you are no longer saving for it. Then you would look at where you expect to be spending (whether that is less, more or the same as before retirement) and add or subtract that number.

For the remainder of this discussion I will be using 70% as the rule of thumb. I have chosen this number for two reasons. First, I am conservative by nature and don't want the stress of feeling like I have to watch every penny during my retirement. And second,

Morneau and Vettese are focused on what Canadian retirees "need." If you've read this far you'll know that I'm focused on what you "want" and most of us want more than we need. And I am willing to sacrifice some of my "wants" now to support the "wants" of my 80-year-old self.

## Less, More, and Same:
## How Much Will You Spend in Retirement?

Once you retire you will likely spend less in some areas, about the same in some, and more in others. For example:

### ▼ Less: Areas where you may spend less in retirement

Ideally, you will have paid off all of your credit card debt by the time you retire, so you don't have to stress about paying off high-interest debt when you're on a fixed income. The same goes for your mortgage. If you can pay it off before you retire, you'll require less because your basic housing costs are covered. You'll probably spend less on your kids—provided that they are done withdrawing from the "Family Bank" for their education and are no longer living at home. You'll probably spend less on work-related expenses like new suits and gas for commuting, and you won't be setting aside part of your paycheque for retirement savings every month, because, well, you'll be retired. You'll also be able to take full advantage of seniors' discounts at all-you-can-eat buffets, provided you're willing to eat dinner at 4pm and buy stretchy pants to accommodate these culinary bargains.

### ➤ Same: Areas where your spending
### may stay the same in retirement

Then there are some areas where you will likely spend about the same in retirement. You'll still have to pay for utilities, the property taxes on your home, and the cost of regular maintenance or condo fees. You'll probably still own a car and be on the hook for upkeep, insurance, and replacement. Many people say that they will "downsize" their home in retirement, but most people don't actually follow through. They may downsize in square footage but buy a condo with expensive maintenance fees, or they may put the money they made from selling their home towards a rental property in the sun.

### ▲ More: Areas where you may spend more in retirement

And finally, there are areas where you will likely spend more in retirement than you did during your working life. This is where you need to flip back and look at the activities that you brainstormed in chapter 2—are these activities going to cost you less than you spent in your working life, about the same, or more? For example, travel tops the list of activities that people want to do when they retire. Instead of the single two-week trip you took every year when you were working, you might want to take an annual extended holiday in a sunnier climate once you're retired. Your hobbies might cost more when you have more time to devote to them as well.

Then there are more mundane areas where you'll likely spend more in retirement. Health care, for instance. As careful as you are to exercise and eat well (and of course you are doing this, right?), health care will cost you more as you age. You might be surprised to learn what the government doesn't cover and how much additional insurance will cost now that you are no longer covered through work. You may also want to protect yourself from a scenario in which you require long-term care—the cost of which can run into thousands of dollars every month.

You will also end up paying more on most products and services you buy, simply because of the ongoing creep of inflation, which runs about 2% per year. This means that a cup of coffee that costs $2 today (a tall, mild blend, no room, if you're buying) will cost about $3.62, thirty years from now. That is a price increase of 81%. For you fancy coffee drinkers, your $5 grande, low-fat, extra-hot latte will cost $9.06 in three decades. See the sidebar for more detail.

~~~~~~~~~~~~~~~~~~~~~~~~~~~~~~~~~~~~~~~~~~~~~~~~~~~~~~

**Q & A**  ## Can Inflation Really Eat My Lunch?

**QUESTION:**

*"I am planning for retirement in twenty years or so and I want to understand how inflation factors in."*

**ANSWER:**

Inflation is the enemy of the retiree. You think bad hips are a problem? You're concerned about predatory door-to-door salesmen or high investment fees? Sure, these are risks. But one of the biggest risks you face when it comes to retirement is inflation. The rising cost of goods and services can really impact your ability to enjoy yourself when you're no longer working.

### Your grocery bill is going up. Way up.

When I was a kid my favourite chocolate bar was a Crispy Crunch. It cost 50 cents. Today you'd be lucky to buy that same chocolate bar for less than $1.50, triple the cost. Because of inflation, prices go up about 2% a year on average. That might not seem like a lot, but because of compounding, it works out to an increase of 81% over three decades. Chocolate bars clearly outpaced the average rate of inflation, but you get the idea.

Take this example: say you spend about $100 on groceries a week. In thirty years that exact same shopping cart of milk, bread, and mangos will cost about $181, simply because of inflation. Ouch.

### The importance of investing

Another way to look at the impact of inflation is that the value of your money declines by about 2% a year because of it. If you left your retirement nest egg in a bank account that earned 0% interest, your purchasing power would decline by 2% every year, or 81% over thirty years. Ouch again. This drives home the point that you need to do two things: save money for retirement and invest that money so that it grows faster than the rate of inflation. Otherwise your purchasing power will decline.

To see how prices have risen over time, you can use the Bank of Canada's inflation calculator (see the link at moolala.ca). The results are pretty shocking.

~~~~~~~~~~~~~~~~~~~~~~~~~~~~~~~~~~~~~~~~~~~~~~~~~~~~

## Calculating How Much Is Enough

So how much do you need to ensure you'll have enough? You can use the super simple "Rule of $20" outlined in the sidebar on page 72. Or, if you have a financial advisor you can ask them to do a detailed calculation for you. This is an area where you can get value from the money you're spending on their advice. Another option is to use an online retirement calculator. So fire up the Internet and I'll walk you through how to do that.

I want to prepare you for a few things before you begin. First, regardless of the calculator you use, you will likely be surprised by the answer it spits out. Not surprised in a "How did you know it was my birthday?" way, but a "Why is there water in my basement?" way. And second, remember that the number is only an estimate, not the "right" answer. There really is no right answer, and, in fact, that isn't the point of the exercise. The point is to have a general sense of how much you'll need in retirement savings. If you don't know what you need, it is impossible to develop a plan to achieve it.

> Regardless of the calculator you use, you will likely be surprised by the answer it spits out.

Note that if you are in a relationship and plan on spending your retirement with that person (not a given, I know), you can calculate your nest egg number together or you can do it separately. I highly recommend doing it together to ensure that you're on the same page and to bring to light any areas of conflict with your current spending habits.

## Consult an Online Retirement Calculator

**GO:** Come on over to moolala.ca and check out one of the retirement calculators we have there, or search online for "retirement calculator." Most of them work in essentially the same way.

**PREP:** In a second, I'm going to ask you to enter your information into the calculator. Before you get started, pull together your most recent RRSP and pension statements, if you have them.

**ENTER:** There are six major areas of information to provide.

**1. AGE:** How old are you now, then, and when you die?

- **Current age**

- **The age you plan to retire**

- **The number of years of retirement:** This is a polite way of asking you the age at which you plan to die—morbid and pretty much impossible to plan, but still important for this calculation. Canadian life expectancy at birth is 79 years for men and 84 years for women. I plan on being around a lot longer than that and want to live comfortably until my number is up. Find out how to estimate your life expectancy in the sidebar at the end of this exercise.

**2. INCOME:** How much will you need to live the life you want?

- **"Target retirement income" or your "annual income desired in retirement."** As I mentioned, the rule of thumb uses a pretty fat thumb. You'll need somewhere between 50% and 100% of the income you earned in your last year of work. I'm talking gross income, as in, before the CRA comes calling for its share. As I said before, I use 70%.

- Generally speaking, the calculators will ask you to state your target retirement income in "today's dollars." That means the calculator will factor in inflation for you. So, if you think you will need $50,000 in income per year in retirement, you input that amount. The calculator will figure out how much $50,000 will actually cost in twenty or thirty years when you are retired.

- It is impossible to predict what you are going to be earning in your last year of retirement, especially if you are still in the early stages of your career. My advice is to take your current salary and double it to account for the salary increases you'll receive over your career. For example, say you're 30 years old and work as an HR coordinator making $30,000 today. In the last year before you retire you could have your boss's job and be making $60,000 per year—twice what you're making now.

3. **PERFORMANCE**: What will your investments return over time?

- Annual rate of return: The retirement calculator might assume a default return value, but you can change it. This variable has a significant impact on your results, so if you want to be conservative, you might use 4% or 5%, and if you want to be more aggressive, you might use 7% or 8%. If you've been following the markets at all over the last decade you have seen that stocks can plummet 40% in one year and jump 40% the next.

- How "conservative" you are, or aren't, isn't just a function of how you feel. It is also a function of time. If you have thirty years until retirement you can afford to take on more risk than someone who has five years until retirement. Great financial advisors will spend the time to understand you and your circumstances to get a sense of your risk tolerance and then recommend investments that are appropriate.

- Some calculators allow you to choose an investment return for your working years and a different one for your retirement. This is because your investments will likely become more conservative the closer you get to withdrawing your money. If you can only input one number, I would recommend you choose something fairly conservative (4% or 5%) so you aren't reliant on huge stock market gains. You might also look at three different assumptions— low at 2%, mid at 5%, and high at 8%—to see how performance will impact your nest egg number over time.

### 4. PENSION PLAN: Do you have one?

- You will be asked if in addition to OAS and CPP you expect to draw some of your retirement income from a Defined Benefit Pension Plan or if you'll be relying on your personal RRSP, Group RRSP or Defined Contribution Pension Plan. (See sidebar for an explanation of these terms and how they fit into this calculation.)

## What Type Of Pension Do You Have?

The first thing to understand is what type of pension you have. Is it a Defined Benefit Pension Plan (DBPP)? Or a Defined Contribution Pension Plan (DCPP)? Or perhaps a Group RRSP?

In a Defined Benefit Pension Plan (DBPP), your employer promises to pay you a set or "defined" *benefit* or income when you retire. The amount is based on a formula that factors in your years of service and your earnings. The DBPP is the pink diamond of pension plans: valuable and rare. (To help you figure out if your DBPP will fund the activities you want to do in retirement, take a look at the exercise on page 78.)

Most employees, if they have anything from work at all, will have a DCPP or Group RRSP. Under a Defined Contribution Pension Plan, it is the *contribution* to the plan that is "defined," both on the part of the employee and the employer. The fixed contribution is usually based on a percentage of the employee's salary and can include an employer match. The amount you'll be able to draw every month in retirement depends on how the assets in your plan increase over time, or, said another way, how large the collective nest egg becomes.

A Group RRSP is very similar to a Defined Contribution Pension Plan, with the main difference being that a DCPP has certain restrictions that "lock in" your money so you can't take it out before normal retirement age—restrictions that the Group RRSP doesn't have. We'll be talking more about Group RRSPs in chapter 8.

The most important thing to understand about the DCPP or Group RRSP is that all risk, both investment risk and longevity risk, is the employee's concern. If the stock market tanks, and your nest egg declines, there will be less money available to you at retirement. And if you live a really long time, there is a chance that the nest egg won't last long enough. For those with a Defined Benefit Pension Plan, it doesn't matter if the stock market tanks, or you live until you're 106 years old because the risk is on the shoulders of the DBPP administrator.

### 5. INFLATION: How fast is the price of coffee going to rise?

- The retirement calculator might assume a default value for inflation, but it is usually adjustable. As I mentioned above, inflation has historically run around 2% per year. If you want to be even more conservative in your calculation, you can choose a number that is slightly higher than that, say 3%.

### 6. RRSPS: What is the status of your RRSP currently?

- **Current value of RRSPs:** You'll want to have a recent RRSP statement at hand so you can include the current value of your RRSPs in your calculation. This would include your personal RRSP, and, if you have a one a Defined Contribution Pension Plan or a Group RRSP from work.

- **Current RRSP contributions:** If you make RRSP contributions, approximately how much are you socking away? And how often—monthly, yearly?

**CALCULATE:** Take a few minutes to check over your answers to these questions. It is super easy to change your answers later, so don't fuss too much this first time around about finding the perfect answer. Once you have input the information, take a deep breath and hit the "calculate" button.

The retirement calculator will use your assumptions to spit out some important numbers. It will give you an estimate of what you will have saved by the time you want to retire. And it will give you an estimate of what you'll need to have saved based on how much you want to spend in retirement. The difference between the two will give you a sense of whether or not you are saving enough for retirement.

**Answer:** According to the online retirement calculator, what is the nest egg number you need to save for your retirement? _____.

And how do you feel about that number? _____.

## Estimating Your Life Expectancy: A Good Time, and Perhaps a Long Time

You cannot know for sure how many years of retirement you need to save for. In my case, it could be a long time. My dad's parents lived until they were 95 and 97, and my mom's parents weren't far behind. I don't know what your family history is, but unless you are an obese asbestos miner with a three-pack-a-day smoking habit and an unwillingness to wear a seat belt, you should be prepared to live into your mid-eighties at the least. If you make it to age 65, Statistics Canada data says you'll likely live another twenty years or so, to age 85. The upside of longevity is, well, you're alive and that's nice. But the downside is that your retirement savings will need to last longer so you finish up before they do.

As morbid as it may seem, estimating how long you might live can be helpful in calculating your retirement savings goal. Online life expectancy calculators such as the *MoneySense* version—cheerfully named "When Will I Die?"—use health and family history data to provide you with the average expiration date for somebody of your height, weight, education, stress level, and history. It can be an illuminating exercise, though not one I'd recommend for birthday or retirement parties. You can find a link to it at moolala.ca.

## Pitfalls to Avoid When Calculating Your Nest Egg Number

Taking the time to figure out a nest egg number for your retirement savings—any number at all—puts you ahead of most people in this country. Well done. I wouldn't be fussed if you simply stopped there, given my strongly held belief that the less complexity you have, the better. However, there are a few pitfalls to be aware of when calculating your number, and for the super keen I will outline them here.

### Neglecting family health history

If you have longevity in your family, you need to plan for it. The same goes for ill health: either of yours or of a family member who may need additional financial support from you after you retire. This could include a relative with special needs or a parent who still needs care after you stop working.

### Underestimating inflation

The overall inflation rate might be just 2% per year, but what about inflation on the things you're going to need as you age? For example, nursing home and assisted living costs have been rising at double the pace of inflation and this trend is likely to continue as the baby boomers get ready to pack their bags and move in.

### Overestimating portfolio performance

Sure, a 7% return has happened in the past, but that is no guarantee that it will happen in the future. This is especially true as you decrease your higher risk equity holdings and increase more conservative fixed income holdings as you age. It is worth checking to see what happens to your estimate if your actual returns come in lower than you predict.

### Deluding yourself about how long you'll work for

I'm part of Generation X and a lot of my peers say that they'll just work longer than their parents did. That might be your intention now, but what if you can't? What if the job prospects for 75-year-olds in your field are bleak? What if you have a health condition that prevents you from doing the same work for the same money that you did at 45? Or what if you're just too damn tired and cranky and "not going to take it anymore!"?

### Tapering spending too aggressively

A lot of people think they will be able to cut expenses significantly once they move out of "active retirement." What they forget is that there is a whole other basket of expenses to consider: medical care not covered by insurance, renovations required to account for mobility issues, and the cost of home care or an assisted living facility. Don't expect that just because you're no longer fit enough to trek the Himalayas that you won't need as much money to live.

### Going into too much detail

Calculating what you need is part science, part science fiction. Remember that you are just coming up with an estimate—your best guess based on what you know now. There is no way to know what the actual number will be. So going into too much detail can lead to overconfidence because you think you've "figured it out."

**Forgetting to update your estimate**

Your nest egg number is ever-changing. Updating your estimate every few years with new information on any of the areas discussed above is really important. Keep notes on the assumptions you made and why you made them so you can see how they change over time.

## The Express Lane: Use the Rule of $20

The "Rule of $20" is one of the simplest methods out there to figure out your nest egg number. The rule was developed by financial services firm Russell Investments and says that you will need $20 saved in your nest egg for every $1 of annual retirement income that you want to have. Say you want to have $100,000 per year in retirement income you will need $2 million saved in your nest egg. The "rule" assumes that your money will need to last about thirty years and accounts for things like inflation, investment performance, and the withdrawals you will make as you start to use part of the nest egg to fund your life. Here is the basic equation:

Target retirement income − CPP and OAS income = nest egg income
Nest egg income × 20 = nest egg required

You start with your target retirement income and subtract the income from CPP and OAS to determine the income you'll need from your nest egg. Then you multiply that number by 20 to give you the size of the nest egg you require.

For example, if you expect to be making $80,000 pre-retirement and want to have 70% of that income available in retirement, your target retirement income is $56,000 ($80,000 × 70%). Then subtract $12,000 (the average you'll get from OAS and CPP combined), and multiply the result ($44,000) by 20. The lump sum required is $880,000. Yep, $880,000.

Check out the table below to see how this works for some other amounts.

**Total nest egg savings required
to achieve target retirement incomes**

| | | | |
|---|---|---|---|
| Target retirement income | $42,000 | $56,000 | $70,000 |
| CPP/OAS income | $12,000 | $12,000 | $12,000 |
| Nest egg income | $30,000 | $44,000 | $58,000 |
| "Rule of $20" | x 20 | x 20 | x 20 |
| Next egg required | $600,000 | $880,000 | $1,160,000 |

There are financial experts who don't like "rules of thumb" in general or the "Rule of $20" in particular. Some of the criticism is about the impact of taxes, but mostly it is about how the rule doesn't factor in people's different circumstances. That's fair. But I would rather you have *a* number, even if it is inaccurate, than no number at all. I see the "Rule of $20" as a starting point—a good way to get people to engage in complex questions without becoming totally overwhelmed.

## Dealing With the Nest Egg Number

Finding out your nest egg number is rarely anyone's favourite exercise. For some people it reaffirms the work they have done so far to save for retirement. But for most people, it is a shocker. Here are some of the comments I've heard after members of the Moolala Community calculated their nest egg numbers.

*"I'm screwed. I'm never going to have enough money to retire."*

*"I'm just going to have to work forever."*

*"There is no way this can be right."*

Stress. Worry. Anger. Disbelief. These reactions are both common and normal. However, rather than wallow in them, I recommend you use the nest egg number as your wake-up call. You have come this far in the *Moolala Guide to Rockin' Your* RRSP and we're soon going to look at how to develop a plan to get your retirement savings on track. There is a lot that you can do, regardless of your age.

If you're in your twenties or thirties, you have time on your side and making some small changes now can make a big difference to your financial future. If you're in your forties and fifties, you will need to move faster and more assertively to get a handle on your retirement savings. And if you're in your sixties, there are still things that you can do to increase the size of your nest egg and, once you retire, to reduce the amount you need to withdraw from it so that it lasts as long as you need it to. Grab a coffee or a cocktail and keep reading. It will be worth the effort, both practically and emotionally. I promise. You might even take some inspiration from this example from the Mooala Community.

*"Divorce hit hard financially a decade ago, but one of the principles I try to live by is to have few regrets. So even though this is a later start than I'd like, I'm thankful to be getting on track with my retirement savings. I've set up a low cost investment plan and enrolled in the Group RRSP at work—something I only recently learned about. The idea of giving money a context made every difference. Mine is "joy." I just got back from vacation in Europe where I found family I had lost track of. I set out with my Dad's 27-year-old address book and not only did I find my cousins and their families, I also found my vision for 'retirement'! I plan to retire near a lake I visited in Hungary, and as an homage to my father, to learn more of the language and obtain dual citizenship. I can't wait to bring my daughters and my grandchildren to visit me there!"*

—Catherine, 56, events planner. Divorced with two grown children and two grandchildren

### Check to See Whether Your Nest Egg Is on Track

You now have a sense of how much money you will need in your nest egg by the time you retire. Now let's see if you're on track to hit that number. If you haven't been contributing regularly to your RRSPs I would predict that this exercise will indicate you are off track. If that's you, and you don't have a pension to factor into the equation, you have my full permission to skip this exercise and leap ahead to page 79 so that you're closer to developing a plan to get a handle on your money. That is coming up soon, I promise.

**FIND:** Stroll on over to moolala.ca and check out the "retirement accumulation calculator" or search for one online.

**ENTER:** You'll be asked about many of the same variables that we addressed in the retirement calculator exercise, in particular your age, investment performance, current RRSP savings, and contribution amount.

**CALCULATE:** The calculator will figure out, based on your current behaviour, what you will have saved by the time you retire and what therefore your annual income will be.

By the time I retire, my savings will be $ _____ (A).
These savings will provide me with an annual income
of $ _____.

**COMPARE:** Write down the nest egg number you came up with previously: $ _____ (B).

Compare number A to number B—that is, compare how much you will have saved by the time you retire with how much you will need to have saved in order to live the life you want. Then answer: Am I on track with my retirement savings? Is A larger than B?

Circle one: **Yes** or **No**

Here is what two members of the Moolala Community found after completing this exercise:

> *"I calculated my nest egg and figured out I need $800,000 by the time I retire. I have $50,000 saved currently and am contributing about $2,400 a year to my RRSP. At this rate I'll have about $370,000 saved by age 65. This will give me an income of $26,000 a year, which I can tell you right now is not going to be enough for me to live on. I need to make some changes."*
> —Sandra, 36, sales rep. Single.

> *"The number the calculator spat out was $1 Million, which I think is insane. But my husband and I have been pretty good about contributing to our RRSPs and if we crank it up a little we will get there on time. It turns out I was worrying about something I didn't need to worry about."*
> —Andrea, 42, consultant. Married with two kids.

You are either on track or you are not. But knowing where you're at now allows you to take action to get back on track.

### Defined Benefit Pension doesn't mean perfection: How much is enough?

If you are one of the fortunate ones who have a Defined Benefit Pension from work, hooray for you. Your retirement savings may be off to a very good start. However, you still need to make sure that pension will be enough to fund your needs and wants in retirement. This is an especially important step if any of the following apply to you: you haven't been earning pension credit for your whole career; your spouse doesn't have a matching pension; you want to retire early; or you want to spend more money in your retirement than you spend today. Here is how some members of the Moolala Community summarized their situations after looking into their pensions in more detail.

*"My pension will ensure I don't starve. But that is about it."*
—Adam, 45, urban planner. Divorced with three teenage kids.

*"I didn't get a 'job' job until my thirties, so I'll only qualify for a pension of about $2,000 per month. That isn't going to be enough to pay for life in retirement, especially given that my wife has been staying at home with the kids and hasn't been saving anything."*
—Bernard, 40, facilities manager. Married with two kids.

*"I put in thirty-five years at my job and earned every cent of my Defined Benefit Pension. It will give me about $3,500 per month after tax. My house is paid off, my kids are financially independent, I am happily single and I am quite content to live a modest life so I don't have to worry about money. I can't see any reason why I'll need to spend much more than $2,500 a month, so I'm really confident that my pension will be enough."*
—Maxine, 62, HR manager. Divorced with two grown children.

*"Technically, yes, it will be enough. But only for me. It doesn't account for my husband and he doesn't have a pension. Plus, this assumes I will continue working with my current employer until retirement, which I myself doubt very highly."*
Farah, 42, software developer. Married with two kids.

If you know you don't have a pension at all, skim this section and move on to page 79. If you do have a pension, pull out one of your recent statements or go onto your company intranet to see whether it is a Defined Benefit or Defined Contribution plan.

I'll wait a minute while you do that.

Seriously. I'm just going to wait right here.

I said a minute. Are you done?

Okay. Good. If you have a Defined Benefit Pension Plan, do the next exercise. And if you have a Defined Contribution Pension Plan you'll already have your nest egg number from the previous exercise.

**EXERCISE**   ## Determine Whether Your DBPP Income Will Exceed Your Expenses

**FIND:** Call your HR department or your pension provider to find out what your pension will provide in income every month when you retire.

**ADD:** Now look at all your expenses and add up what those expenses are now and what you expect they'll be in retirement. As mentioned above, you'll spend less on some things, the same on some, and more on others. Do the simplest version of this calculation, or, if you have one, ask your financial advisor to do it with you. Will your retirement expenses be 50%, or half, of what you spend today? Or do you predict your expenses will be more like 100%, meaning that you expect to spend in retirement about what you spend today?

**CALCULATE:** Take your estimated retirement income and subtract your estimated expenses to see if there will be a surplus or a deficit. Of course a deficit means that you should be saving more in addition to your pension to ensure that you'll have enough money in retirement. And a surplus means that, based on this math at least, you'll have a bit of money left over to spend at the snack bar of your retirement home.

**ANSWER:** Summarize your calculations by answering this question: based on my estimated Defined Benefit Pension income and retirement expenses will I have enough to retire?

Circle one: **Yes** or **No**

Sure, there's a chance that your expected pension will provide you with all you want in retirement. You worked hard for that pension, so if this is the case, consider yourself very fortunate. But you may find that there is a gap between what your pension will provide and what you will want to spend in retirement. If that's the case you'll need to save more inside an RRSP or a Tax-Free Savings Account (TFSA) to top up your nest egg.

Even if you feel confident that your Defined Benefit Pension Plan is going to be enough, you might still consider some additional savings. Why? To give you additional security, keep your options open and protect you against inflation.

Enviable pension or not, you might find yourself wishing you'd socked some of your mad money away for a rainy day.

## What Are Some Unconventional Ways to Fund My Retirement?

**QUESTION:**

*"I have always been skeptical about RRSPs and so have contributed very little over the years. I'm single and now on the verge of retirement. I don't have a company pension, but my kids are out of the house and my mortgage is paid off. What are my options for retirement?"*

**ANSWER:**

AHHHHHHHHHHHH!

I don't mean to add to your level of anxiety, but if you are on the verge of retirement and haven't saved at all, you are in a tough situation. And while I could try to speak soothingly about easy ways to solve this problem, there are no easy answers.

Most of the time we talk about "saving for" retirement. In this case, we need to focus on "funding" your retirement, given that you are about to end your working life and enter this new phase without a steady source of income. The most obvious thing to recommend is that you continue to work as long as you can, to build up the biggest possible nest egg for when you really need it. If you aren't able to do that you will need to carefully manage your income and expenses so that you can pay for the basics.

Your financial base will be OAS and CPP. Depending on your CPP contributions during your career, the two combined will give you somewhere around $12,000 per year. This won't go far when it comes to paying for utilities, property taxes, and other day-to-day essentials. So how can you increase your income or cut your expenses to fund your retirement? I have a few ideas, but I don't expect you to like any of them because they all involve making some significant trade-offs.

**Sell your house and downsize early**

Many seniors talk about their house being their retirement fund. As I mentioned in chapter 1, this only really works if you sell your home and put the money to work generating income so you have money to put groceries in your fridge. Sure, you could get a reverse mortgage, but the fees are high and you are still living in a house that you can't afford.

Instead of waiting until you're 75 years old, consider downsizing now. And when I say "downsize" I mean in dollars, not just square footage. Say you can sell your house for $500,000 and then buy something smaller and in a more affordable neighbourhood for $300,000. This frees up $200,000 that you can put to work in something that generates an income, like dividend-paying stocks or bonds. Interest rates are at a record low these days, but at least you'll get something deposited into your bank account each month. You likely don't want to sell your house, for a myriad of reasons, but this isn't about what you want to do, it is about what you need to do.

**Develop a source of passive income**

To increase your cash flow you can either increase income or cut expenses. Once you retire, you could develop a source of passive income. People with greater resources and expertise might look at buying a rental property or starting a business. But in your case, I would keep it simple and consider renting out part of your home— for example, creating a basement suite or taking in a boarder.

### Move to a lower-cost region or country

You can make your money go further by spending less of it. The wild idea would be to move to a lower-cost country, like Panama or Nicaragua. But if you can't bear to work through the tax and health care issues or don't want to brush up on your Spanish, consider moving to a lower-cost community within Canada. For example, Elliott Lake, Ontario, has been marketing itself to seniors for years, focusing on high quality of life for a low cost. If you can dramatically cut your cost of living, you can stretch your limited income further.

### Cut living costs dramatically

Moving might be too difficult for you. Instead, how could you cut your living expenses significantly while staying in town? Could you sell your car or cut off cable, phone, and magazine subscriptions? Could you trim maintenance or grocery costs? We'll talk more in chapter 15 about sustainable spending and what might be a strategy for you.

### Rely on your kids

You think I'm joking. I'm not joking. Another option is to talk to your kids now about how they can help with your expenses in your retirement. Or ask them if they will have the financial resources to provide you with some sort of income stipend. I know a family that has both grandmothers living with them. This isn't a common practice in Canada these days, but in many cultures it is. And it might work for you.

As I said, I don't expect you to love any of these ideas, but I encourage you to think about unconventional ways to increase income (legally) and cut your expenses so that you're able to fund your life once you are no longer working.

## Behind Door Number One:
## A Look at Three Different Retirement Scenarios

We have spent a good amount of time on what you'd like your retirement to actually look like and how much that retirement will actually cost. I wanted to leave the numbers behind for a moment and paint a picture of what three different retirement scenarios might look like, depending on the saving you do before you stop drawing a paycheque. Behind door number one...

### 1. NO-SAVE RETIREMENT

In this first scenario, let's pretend you made a decision not to save a dime for your retirement. You paid into the Canada Pension Plan for decades without having compromised your lifestyle one iota while you were working—you spent time with your kids, feathered your nest a bit and loved every minute of it. At 65, you are content to reap your CPP and OAS benefits. However, you are no longer with your spouse so there is no one to split the bills with. Here's what your no-save retirement might look like:

- **Annual income:** $24,000, before tax. Half of this amount, $12,000, comes from the approximately $1,000 per month that you'll receive from OAS and CPP. The remaining $12,000 comes from interest on the lump sum you will receive when you sell your house.

- **Gimme shelter:** There's no way you could have afforded to pay the property tax and substantial utility bills that came with your family home. You've thus sold the house, paid off your debt with the profits, invested the remaining proceeds and now rent a six-hundred-square-foot apartment. That wasn't easy to swallow, but there was no other way to significantly reduce your monthly expenses and provide a bit of a nest egg to put groceries in your fridge. You have invested the money conservatively and predict it will last for thirty years.

- **Getting around:** You won't be able to own a vehicle—gas and insurance payments alone would eat up 10% to 15% of your monthly income, never mind repairs—but public transit is more accessible than ever and, at long last, you qualify for the seniors' discount on a bus pass. There's also car sharing and carpooling when you're in a pinch.

- **Parks and recreation:** While you used to picture your retired self as one of those Zenned-out silver-haired types on the "Freedom 55" brochure, wearing Bermuda shorts and golfing in, well, Bermuda, that's not the reality of your retirement phase. Now the absolute best thing you can do for yourself is this: own it. Accept your reality. Make friends with your retirement. This was your choice and it's your life; wishing and coveting and gazing at those shiny clubs in the window of Golf Town will only make you nuts. You could afford to get into jogging—try guided group walks or runs at the Running Room, which are free at 8:30 a.m. every Sunday across the country. You might also immerse yourself in volunteer work, write that book you always wanted to write, or learn to program HTML.

- **Take flight:** In terms of visiting far-flung locales to see your children and grandchildren, you've devoted yourself to collecting Air Miles, and you plan extended stays when you do visit every few years (you're considering borrowing *The Good Granny Guide* from the library to learn how to not become an annoyance for those six-week-long sojourns).

- **In short:** The no-save retirement plan has ensured you are rooted locally and your now limited choices are clear-cut. Still, with some seriously creative planning, a no-frills retirement can be active and fulfilling.

### 2. MID-RANGE RETIREMENT

If the first scenario doesn't suit you, you may instead choose to put enough in your RRSP to leave yourself at least 50% of your $80,000 income annually during your retirement phase. I'll call this the mid-range retirement:

- **Annual income:** $40,000 including OAS and CPP, before tax.

- **Gimme shelter:** At this level, you can consider keeping your mortgage-free house or selling it to move into a nice condo (again, you'll reap far greater benefit by doing that before you retire). You could earmark your CPP payments for condo fees, property tax, and utility bills if you choose a roomier townhouse.

- **Getting around:** You have to downgrade your VW Touareg to a more affordable Toyota Matrix, but that's hardly a hardship.

- **Parks and recreation:** On $40,000 you could continue to indulge in many of your favourite pastimes: hiking in the nearby mountains, skiing locally all winter, golfing locally all summer and entertaining friends and family with dinners and brunches on a regular basis. With one eye on your budget, you will continue to take pleasure in buying reasonable gifts for kids and grandkids.

- **Take flight:** Unless there's some expensive car- or house-related emergency, you can usually afford a week-long scuba vacation every year or perhaps once every two years if you want to also make annual visits to your kids on the coast.

- **In short:** All in all, your retirement is relaxing. You can breathe easy and live the life you want without making many painful changes in the day-to-day.

### 3. HIGH-END RETIREMENT

In theory, everyone wants a deluxe retirement. It is possible, but it will take more sacrifice now in terms of what you put into your RRSP; if living the high(ish) life is the only path you can tolerate, you may have some catching up to do. Let's say you save a nest egg that is large enough to give yourself 70% of your current salary every year. Here's what a high-end retirement might look like:

- **Annual income:** $56,000 including OAS and CPP, before tax.

- **Gimme shelter:** At $56,000 per year, you can either stay in your beloved family home or move into that 1,200-square-foot condo near the water that you've had your eye on.

- **Getting around:** Keep your car or even upgrade a little if that turns your crank.

- **Parks and recreation:** You can buy all the Bermuda shorts you like and even spend a few weeks a year wearing them during the winter (and I don't mean in that crazy-Canuck sort of way—I mean on beaches with umbrellas in your drinks). A gym membership is no problem, and neither is a reasonably priced golf membership (after all, while you're very comfortable, you're not Donald Trump thank your lucky stars for that). Alternatively, you finally have the time to build that adobe bread oven in the backyard, take courses, and gleefully buy all the supplies you need (a weekend in San Francisco to sample the walnut loaf may be in order). You can host wine-infused dinner parties for your friends once a month without breaking a sweat (except in the kitchen).

- **Take flight:** Most important to you, perhaps, you have enough cash to visit your kids in Montreal or Moose Jaw once a year plus in between if there's a special graduation or birthday.

- **In short:** Life is full and fun. Best of all, with little restraint, you have as many choices as—and certainly more time than—when you were working full-time.

## Conclusion

It often doesn't feel like you have choices when it comes to retirement savings. And while there is no shortage of competition for every dollar you have, you do have choices in terms of what you save and what you spend. And those choices will determine what your life looks like a few decades from now. Step 2 of the Moolala Method was about building on your knowledge of retirement savings by determining how much you need for your particular version of that life stage. You calculated how large a nest egg you will need and whether you are on track to achieve it. For many of you that number was daunting, if not downright depressing. But don't stop now. Step 3 is all about developing the plan to help you get the retirement you want. Let's go.

# STEP 3

---

# DEVELOP
# THE PLAN

---

STEP 1 > STEP 2 > STEP 3 > STEP 4 > STEP 5
Lay the | Determine | Develop | Take | Stay
foundation | how much | the plan | action | engaged
 | you need

# { 6 }

## WHAT'S THE PLAN, STAN?
### COME UP WITH ONE
### THAT WILL WORK FOR YOU

---

THERE ARE a number of things that one gains with age. Wisdom is one, for sure, and hooray for that. However, in my case at least, I gained something else along with my wisdom: weight.

I was pear-shaped as a preteen, and slimmed as I grew up. But as an adult I was reverting to the pear, and I didn't like what I saw. I exercised some, but not enough to offset my high-calorie, high-carb vices. Clearly I needed a plan. My friend Guy suggested a book called *Body for Life*, and he promised to follow the plan with me for three months. I was totally embarrassed when I picked it up at the bookstore. The "before and after" pictures and outlandish promises were laughable as was the simplistic and poorly written self-help rah-rah. But it was a pretty simple plan and I committed to following it—eating six small meals a day and doing the exercises it touted.

And you know what?

It worked. In three months I trimmed right up, just as the toothy, fake-bake-tanned bodybuilder on the cover said I would.

Getting what you want is easier with a plan. I have learned from experience that it doesn't so much matter *what* the plan is; what matters is simply having a plan at all.

Step 1 and Step 2 of the Moolala Method focused on building your knowledge about retirement savings, your needs and wants, and how much you'll need to pay for it all. In Steps 3, 4, and 5 we are going to shift our focus towards developing a few important skills. First among them is the skill of creating a plan to get a handle on your retirement savings. The plan will cover a number of different actions, outlined below. You may have already completed some of these things. Go you! Here is what we are going to cover, to help you choose your wine cellar and get it stocked up.

**Develop the Plan and Take Action**

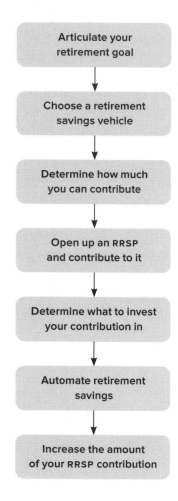

Articulate your retirement goal

Choose a retirement savings vehicle

Determine how much you can contribute

Open up an RRSP and contribute to it

Determine what to invest your contribution in

Automate retirement savings

Increase the amount of your RRSP contribution

## { 7 }

# ARTICULATE YOUR
# RETIREMENT GOAL
## SUMMARIZE THE WHEN,
## WHY, AND HOW MUCH

---

IN THE previous chapter you did the math to figure out what your nest egg will need to be for you to afford the retirement you want. Now I'm going to ask you to summarize that work in a super simple, clear way that states when you want to retire, how much you will need, and why it is important to you.

It is appropriate for you to be a little skeptical about this part. "Really? I'm really talking about retirement in this level of detail when it is thirty years, maybe forty years, in the future?" I know. Crazy, right? But trust me. It works. It will help shift the idea of your retirement from something that only old people need to think about to something that is relevant to you now, so you'll be more motivated to start saving.

For those of you who maintain that you'll never retire, please flip back to the "myths and misconceptions" section in chapter 1 and then come back to me. It may well be true that you will never retire, but you don't want to depend on that, in case it simply isn't possible for you to emulate the career longevity of Joan Rivers.

This retirement goal is just a starting point. As the years unfold you might change the age at which you plan to retire—moving it earlier or later. How much you need might change too as you get a better sense of what you want to do in retirement, and how much money you will actually have. Your "why," or the context for your retirement savings, may evolve with time as well. But it is much easier to modify a goal than to try to develop a plan with no goal in the first place.

Here is an example of one retirement goal from the Moolala Community:

*"When: 65 years old.*

*How much: $800,000 nest egg.*

*Why: Travel. When it comes to retirement, my money is for travel."*

Now it's your turn.

---

 **Articulate Your Retirement Goal**

**PONDER:**

- **When:** How old will you be when you retire?

- **How much:** How much do you need to pay for it?

- **Why:** Why is it important to you to save for retirement? This is the "context" for retirement savings that we talked about in chapter 2. When it comes to retirement, my money is for _____.

**WRITE:** Fill in the blanks below.

My retirement goal:

When: _____

How much: _____

Why: _____

**COPY:** Copy this retirement goal down onto a piece of paper and put it somewhere you can easily read it a few times a year. Perhaps that's in the file where you keep your financial papers. Or set up a recurring appointment in your online calendar so that it will pop up every few months.

**TALK:** Have one conversation about this retirement goal with some-one in your life—your spouse, a friend, a sibling, or your financial advisor—to clarify it in your mind. Take them through the three parts of the goal and then talk a bit about how you feel when you review the goal. It is also a good idea to talk about the activities you'd like to do in retirement, as absurd as that may seem, because we are more motivated to take action on something that is real. If it makes you more comfortable, as you start the conversation, roll your eyes and say in your best, bored teenage voice, something like, "I'm read-ing this personal finance book. It has the weirdest title ever, *Moolala*. Anyway, I'm trying to do the exercises—even if they are dumb—and this is one of them." Then roll your eyes again.

## Conclusion

Now that you have articulated your retirement goal you have a des-tination towards which you can orient yourself. Sure, it may change along the way—perhaps dramatically—but at least you know in which direction to start walking.

## { 8 }

# CHOOSE A RETIREMENT
# SAVINGS VEHICLE

## UNDERSTAND TFSAS, GROUP RRSPS, AND SPOUSAL RRSPS

---

**Y**OU NOW have a sense of what you want for your retirement, as vague and far in the future as it may be. So let's talk about how you're going to get it.

In chapter 4 we went through the "who, what, when, where and how" of RRSPs, and highlighted the benefits they offer of tax deferral and tax-free growth. (Oh yeah—and the tax refund you'll likely get, which you will put towards credit card debt and *not* a trip to Cuba.) In addition to the RRSP there is also the "Tax-Free Savings Account" or TFSA, which has been receiving a lot of attention lately. Some people use it to save for retirement, though it's not for everyone. We'll look at the TFSA in more detail below.

In addition to the RRSP and TFSA there are a few other options that you might use in combination—a Group RRSP, a Defined Contribution Pension Plan, and a spousal RRSP. We'll cover each of these as we work through developing a plan, and then we'll have you choose the retirement savings vehicle (or combination of vehicles) that is right for you.

## The Basics of TFSAs

Introduced in 2009, the TFSA is relatively new to Canadians. If you're confused about what it is and how it works, you are in good company. Here are the basics:

**WHAT:** Like an RRSP, a TFSA is also a special wine cellar, but it works in a different way. The money you contribute to a TFSA is not tax deductible, so, unlike an RRSP, a TFSA contribution doesn't reduce your taxable income. So your contribution is made with "after-tax" dollars, but the money you contribute grows tax-free, hence the name. If you were to just put the money into a regular savings account you would have to pay tax on whatever income you earned. TFSAs are a great savings vehicle for many different purposes—a new car, vacation, the down payment on a house, and in some cases, retirement, though it wasn't designed specifically as a retirement savings account the way RRSPs were. More on that below.

> TFSAs are a great savings vehicle for many different purposes—a new car, vacation, the down payment on a house, and in some cases, retirement.

**WHERE:** You can set up a TFSA at a bank, credit union, discount broker, full-service broker, or mutual fund company. Some types of TFSAs function only as savings accounts and others allow you to hold a full range of investments, such as a mutual fund, exchange-traded fund, stock, bond, or GIC. You may also be able to open a TFSA through your employer—allowing you to set up payroll deductions that deposit money directly into your TFSA.

**HOW MUCH:** If you were at least 18 years old in 2009, the year the TFSA was introduced, you've been accumulating $5,000 in contribution room every year since. The amount is indexed to inflation, to the closest $500, so the limit since 2013 has been $5,500. You don't have to open a TFSA to start building contribution room—it just grows whether you want it to or not—and the unused contribution room is carried forward. So if you open your first TFSA in 2014 you'll be allowed to deposit $31,000 into it right away. As with an RRSP, you don't want to deposit more than you're allowed, as the Canada Revenue Agency will penalize you. The table below illustrates how total contribution room within a TFSA grows over time.

**TFSA contribution limits**

| YEAR | ANNUAL LIMIT | TOTAL CONTRIBUTION ROOM |
|------|--------------|-------------------------|
| 2009 | $5,000 | $5,000 |
| 2010 | $5,000 | $10,000 |
| 2011 | $5,000 | $15,000 |
| 2012 | $5,000 | $20,000 |
| 2013 | $5,500 | $25,500 |
| 2014 | $5,500 | $31,000 |
| 2015 | $5,500 | $36,500 |
| 2016 | $5,500 | $42,000 |

**HOW:** You transfer money into your TFSA account and then invest it how you like. You could leave it in cash, or buy some sort of an investment with the money, say a mutual fund, exchange-traded fund, stock, bond, or GIC.

**WHEN:** TFSAS are very flexible and there isn't an annual deadline like there is with an RRSP. There are certain restrictions about withdrawing and then re-depositing money into a TFSA, but your banker can help you sort all that out.

**WHO:** Anyone who is over age 18 and has a social insurance number can open up a TFSA. Unlike an RRSP you don't have to have "earned income" in order to contribute.

## Retirement Savings Match-Up:
## The RRSP versus the TFSA

One of my favourite songs is called "RRSPs are the best." I sing it morning, noon and night, to anyone and everyone, young and old. I'm almost a one-hit wonder when it comes to the best way to save for retirement.

Almost. But not entirely.

### Modest Income Earners: The TFSA might be for you

The big wow of contributing to an RRSP is that it allows you to defer income tax to a point in the future when you are no longer drawing a paycheque and will presumably be in a lower tax bracket. For people in the modest income category, say those making under $45,000 a year, there is less to be gained from the tax deferral of an RRSP because you are already in a low tax bracket and not likely to be in a lower one when you retire.

> One of my favourite songs is called "RRSPs are the best." I sing it morning, noon and night, to anyone and everyone, young and old.

In fact, drawing from an RRSP might put you in a higher tax bracket than when you were working if you are collecting the full amounts on CPP, OAS, and GIS. (Refer back to chapter 5 for an explanation of the Canada Pension Plan, Old Age Security, and Guaranteed Income Supplement.)

If you earn less than $45,000 per year, it could make more sense to save what you can for retirement in a Tax-Free Savings Account. Given that your contributions to a TFSA will be made with after-tax money, there will be no tax to pay when you withdraw that money from the account down the road. Besides, if you have a modest income, the $5,500 contribution limit won't be that constraining to your retirement savings. If you have a higher income, that limit will be too small. Let's say you earn $80,000 a year and want to put away 18% of your income, or $14,400, for retirement. The TFSA won't give you the room, but the RRSP will.

**I'm a Low-Paid Academic.
Should I Worship at the RRSP Altar?**

**QUESTION:**

*"I have a Ph.D. but have been having a tough time finding a well-paying job. For the past year and a half I have been making do with part-time work and have a very low income. That being said, I am frugal and have maxed out my TFSA and invested in some low-fee funds in a non-registered account. I am wondering whether it is a good idea for me to transfer these non-registered investments into an RRSP at present or to keep waiting until I secure a well-paying job."*

**ANSWER:**

I can only imagine how impatient you must be to get moving on your career. The Kraft Dinner diet works for a while, but then your stomach grumbles for something a little more substantial. Impatience on the work front will serve you well, provided that you can channel it towards the schmoozing, applying, and interviewing that a job search requires. But at this point in time you don't need to be impatient about saving for retirement. Contributions to your RRSP can wait, for now.

**Wait for a higher tax bracket to transfer money**

You are already in a low tax bracket because of your modest income, so you have much less of a need to defer income tax. Transferring those investments into an RRSP will generate a tax refund, but you're better off waiting until you're in a higher tax bracket to do so, when you'll receive a bigger tax refund for the same size of contribution. (It is worth noting that you could transfer the money to your RRSP now and then carry forward the deduction to a future year— but that seems like a lot of work at this point.)

### Take advantage of financial flexibility

What is awesome about your story is that you have finished your studies without a keg full of debt, and you have savings in the bank. If you found a job in some far-flung land, you would be able to take it because you have the $10,000 you would need to move to another city. And your non-registered investments could go towards the down payment on a home if you got a tenure track position somewhere, or a reliable used car to get to your great new job.

Transferring your savings to an RRSP will reduce your flexibility. While you'd be able to cash it out later on, there would be a tax hit and it isn't as simple to do as with a TFSA. It is better to continue saving what you can, and wait until you have some certainty about where you'll be living and what you'll be earning before you put the money in an RRSP.

### Maintain strong savings habits regardless of income

Your frugal behaviour has clearly served you well in these lean times, as demonstrated by the fact that you have a maxed-out TFSA and a non-registered account with something in it. Which is the third reason why I think you can wait to transfer those investments into an RRSP. You already have the habit ingrained, and the sad reality is that most people don't.

Keep doing what you're doing, and when the income you seek starts to flow you'll be able to build your retirement savings at a pretty nice clip.

Good luck to you.

### Defined Benefit Pension Plan Recipients: Check out the TFSA

The second category of people for whom a TFSA can make more sense than an RRSP are those who have a Defined Benefit Pension Plan. This is the kind of pension where your employer promises to pay you a set income when you retire. There are a few reasons a TFSA might make more sense for these people.

**Tax bracket in retirement:** RRSPS give you an up-front tax refund, which is beneficial in the short run, and often beneficial in the long run if you're in a lower tax bracket in retirement. But what if you aren't? If your years of service have earned you a rich pension in retirement you may find that your income doesn't fall that much when you retire, so the lower tax bracket benefit you're banking on with an RRSP is less likely. If this describes your situation, you might be better off saving additional money inside a TFSA. That money will already be "after-tax," so when you withdraw it you won't be paying income tax on the money. That being said, the TFSA doesn't provide nearly as much contribution room as the RRSP, so that may be a constraint.

**The benefit of flexibility:** If you believe that your pension income will be sufficient to fund your retirement you might not need to save more in an RRSP. Money that is held in an RRSP is more costly and difficult to access than if it was in a TFSA because you pay tax on withdrawals. So, instead of, or in addition to, contributing to an RRSP you could save some money in a TFSA and use it how and when you see fit—on travel, renovations, a new car or gifts to adorable grandchildren. Remember, however, that you will still need to check that your pension is going to be enough to fund the retirement you want to have, as we discussed in the previous chapter.

There is one important caveat here: If you have a Defined Benefit Pension Plan from the government, you can have a fairly high level of confidence that you'll be paid. But unlike death and taxes, a pension isn't 100% guaranteed, particularly in the private sector. If you need proof, just ask a retired employee of Nortel Networks—I'm sure they will be more than willing to provide you with a cautionary tale.

Note that there is one other group of people for whom the TFSA makes sense for retirement savings. If you have used up all of your RRSP contribution room, a TFSA is a good place to park additional savings.

**RRSPs and TFSAs: A side-by-side comparison**

| | RRSP | TFSA |
|---|---|---|
| Primary purpose | Retirement savings | Saving for anything |
| Age of eligibility | No minimum age | Must be age of majority (18 or 19, depending on your province) |
| Plan maturity | End of the year you turn 71 | No maximum age |
| Annual contribution limit | 18% of previous year's earned income, up to a maximum | $5,500 ($5,000 for the years 2009 to 2012) |
| Earned income | Required | Not required |
| Contributions | Tax-deductible | Not tax-deductible |
| Unused contribution room | Carried forward | Carried forward |
| Growth | Tax-deferred (not taxed until withdrawal) | Tax-free (never taxed) |
| Withdrawals | Taxable | Tax-free |

 **Q & A**  **My Kid Is Too Young to Drive. But Is He Too Young for an RRSP?**

**QUESTION:**

*"Can my fourteen-year-old son start an RRSP? Or is a TFSA a better place to start?"*

**ANSWER:**

Yes, your son *can* start an RRSP. And more importantly, he *should*. All kids should. Their part-time jobs will give them the earned income they need to enable them to contribute to an RRSP, and the benefits are huge. Here is why I'm so passionate about RRSPs for kids, young people, and even not-so-young people.

- **Ingrain the habit of long-term saving:** The biggest benefit of starting an RRSP so young is that your son will develop a really useful habit: saving for retirement. Remember when I said getting a handle on your money was a function of knowledge, skills, and habits? Saving for retirement is one of the most important habits. Sure, the amount he contributes will fluctuate over the years because of school expenses, mortgage payments, or even kids of his own. But he will be used to putting something aside every year for retirement, even if it is $100. If your son starts contributing now, before peer pressure on spending really takes hold, there is a higher probability that he'll be able to stick with the habit over time. Ingraining the RRSP habit is the key, and it is more important than the amount of the contribution itself.

- **Make compounding count:** Your son has time on his side, and the earlier he starts saving for retirement, the easier it will be to reach his ultimate goal because he'll keep earning interest on his interest. The TFSA is a great place to save for shorter-term goals like a house or a car. But the RRSP is better for retirement, in part because it is harder to take the money out. He is more likely to leave it in and benefit from compound interest over the next four or five decades. As you know, one hundred dollars socked away at age 15 is going to grow more significantly than that same hundred dollars deposited at age 30.

- **RRSPs still provide some flexibility:** If your son decides that he wants to borrow some money from his RRSP to put towards a down payment on his first house through the Home Buyers' Plan or to fund further education through the Lifelong Learning Plan, he can do that. He can also contribute to his RRSP now but choose when he wants to actually take advantage of the tax deferral, either now or when he's earning more money and therefore in a higher tax bracket.

Now, not everyone agrees that RRSPs are great for kids, just so you know. The basic argument against RRSPs for young people like your son is that he is in a low tax bracket now and will likely be at a higher one in the future, so the tax deferral will be more valuable then. This is true. But your son can simply contribute to an RRSP now and wait to take the tax deduction when he is making more money in the future.

Sure, your son could open up a TFSA for more short-term goals in addition to an RRSP, but I would highly recommend that his first priority be to open an RRSP with an automatic withdrawal set up every pay day, moving money from his bank account to his RRSP.

Was that too subtle an answer? Should I spell it out? Registered Retirement Savings Plan. Start there.

## I'm President and CEO of Me Inc. What Is My Best Retirement Savings Strategy?

**QUESTION:**

*"I've just started my own business. Should I be doing anything different when it comes to retirement savings?"*

**ANSWER:**

You're in very good company—these days more and more people are running their own businesses, either because they love the flexibility and control it can offer or because they can't find full-time work and have to pay the bills through contract work instead. It is even more important for someone in your situation to be thinking about retirement because of the risks entrepreneurship involves. I have a few tips for you here and I'd recommend you also read the "volatile income" sidebar in chapter 14.

### Invest in a consultation with an accountant

I know that sounds like a total cop-out but I don't mean it to be. There are just too many issues beyond the scope of this guide that will impact your approach: for example, choosing to incorporate or run a sole proprietorship, determining which business expenses to write off, employing family members, ensuring that your work with clients doesn't constitute an "employer-employee relationship." You get the idea. Retirement savings and tax planning are inextricably linked for those who own their own business, and a trained and experienced accountant can help you sort through what will be best for you.

### Pay yourself in dividends

I do have one retirement strategy that many small business owners aren't aware of: paying yourself in dividends versus salary. How this works is that you incorporate your business, then keep all of the profits inside your business, except for what you need to live on. Those living expenses are paid in the form of dividends, which are taxed at a lower rate than a salary. And you will not have to pay into CPP, which will keep more money in your pocket. This strategy generally makes sense if taxable income from the business will be more than $50,000 per year, and you are confident that you'll be able to leave a reasonable surplus in the corporation as savings.

Note that because you won't be paid a salary and you won't be contributing to CPP, you'll receive less money from the government in retirement. And you won't be generating "earned income" so you won't build up RRSP contribution room either. That means you need to make sure that you save money inside the corporation to fund your retirement. The retained earnings in your corporation become your retirement nest egg and you will need to invest it well. Then, after you retire you will be able to continue to withdraw dividends from the corporation to pay for your great life. Again, talk to an accountant to see if this makes sense for you.

### Think about your exit strategy

You should also think how you can exit the business at or before retirement in the most profitable way. This strategy, done well, could form an important part of your retirement savings plan either in the form of a lump sum or a percentage of revenue that you earn over time. Building a business that you can sell is difficult, especially when you are providing a service. Clients come to expect that you'll be the one to deliver that service, so they'll need to become accustomed to your replacement. And it can be really tough to find a buyer who has the right skills and an appetite for entrepreneurial risk who is interested in buying you out. Be sure to develop your exit strategy 5 to 10 years before you want it to happen. It may be that selling your business is an unrealistic goal and instead you need to be focused on saving for your retirement in the good old-fashioned way—building a nest egg filled with investments that you can draw from over time.

## Other Types of RRSPs

We covered off the standard-issue RRSP in chapter 4, and for many of you that will suffice. But there are two other types of RRSPs that are worth mentioning: the Group RRSP and the spousal RRSP. At least skim through these sections in case any of it applies to you or someone you love—because if they fit your circumstances these RRSPs may be helpful when it comes to saving for retirement.

### Group RRSPs: Becoming a groupie

More isn't always merrier when you think of hot tubs, jalapeños or visits from your in-laws. But in the case of RRSPs it most definitely is. If the company you work for offers a Group RRSP plan to employees, run, don't walk, to your human resources office to sign up *tout de suite*. A Group RRSP can help you build a bigger nest egg for your retirement, and that will make you merrier indeed.

A Group RRSP is basically a collection of individual RRSPs offered to employees by their sponsoring employer. It is similar to a Defined Contribution Pension Plan, with the main difference being that a DCPP has restrictions on it that "lock in" your money so you can't take it out before normal retirement age. A Group RRSP is not generally as rich as a Defined Benefit Pension Plan, but it does provide a number of benefits.

### "Match" your way to a million bucks

Most companies that offer Group RRSPs also offer to "match" some or all of their employee's contributions usually up to a maximum percentage of the employee's salary. Let's say you contribute 6% of your salary to your employer's Group RRSP. If they have a generous program they could match your contribution 100%, adding another 6% of your salary to your RRSP. Sure, like a traditional bonus, the money is taxable, but it's free money. And because the "bonus" is paid inside your RRSP, the tax is deferred anyway. Said another way, you'll pay the tax on your T4, but then your RRSP contribution receipt offsets the taxable portion.

Here are three scenarios using employees at the same company who earn the same amount of money:

- **Average salary:** $70,000 per year
- **Employer match:** 100% up to 6% of salary
- **Investment return:** 5%
- **Time:** 40 years

**MARCUS:** He doesn't participate in the Group RRSP. He may or may not save elsewhere for retirement, but he doesn't take advantage of this employee benefit.

**PRAVEEN:** She participates in the Group RRSP but only signs up for a 3% contribution, therefore earning a 3% match, when she is eligible for a 6% match.

**VIRGINIA:** She is rocking her Group RRSP. She signs up for a 6% contribution and qualifies for the full 6% match. She saves a nest egg of $522,000 by herself—double what Praveen put away—and also gets another $522,000 from her employer. Her nest egg is worth over a million dollars after 40 years, double what it would have been if she'd only signed up for a 3% contribution. Said another way, Virginia received a whopping $522,000 bonus from the company, a guaranteed return of 100%. Praveen received just $261,000 and Marcus got nothing but a gold-plated watch.

**Three Group RRSP scenarios**

|  | MARCUS: 0% | PRAVEEN: 3% | VIRGINIA: 6% |
|---|---|---|---|
| Annual employee contribution | – | $2,100 | $4,200 |
| Annual employer match | – | $2,100 | $4,200 |
| Total employee contribution | – | $261,000 | $522,000 |
| Total employer match | – | $261,000 | $522,000 |
| Total retirement nest egg | – | $522,000 | $1,044,000 |

**Group RRSP participation rates suck, for no good reason**

Here is the crazy thing: many people who are eligible to participate in a Group RRSP either don't participate at all, or don't take advantage of the full employer match. Not participating at all is simply inexcusable, even if you find the forms jargony and complicated. This is akin to taking a portion of your paycheque, in cash, and handing it over to your accounts payable clerk to deposit back into your employer's bank account. Who does that? And you should participate even if you don't think you'll be with your employer very long. I'll cover off what happens to your money in the next sidebar.

Not taking full advantage of a Group RRSP is easier to understand early in your career, given all the other demands you have on your money, especially when your salary is still low. But it isn't smart: You are missing out on an amazing payoff, and are quite likely to forget to call up HR to increase your contribution rate to the maximum level as your salary climbs.

**Many people who are eligible to participate in a Group RRSP either don't participate at all, or don't take advantage of the full employer match.**

### Lower fees than regular mutual funds

The second benefit of a Group RRSP is that you may be able to save on management fees. We'll talk more about fees later in the guide, but what is relevant here is that your employer will likely be able to negotiate a lower fee than you would pay if you invested in mutual funds on your own. This can boost the performance of your investments dramatically over time.

### A "work around" for weak willpower

Participating in a Group RRSP gives you money you wouldn't have otherwise received in the form of an employer "match" and allows you to invest that money at what could be a lower cost than investing it in mutual funds by yourself. The third benefit of a Group RRSP is they are a great work-around for weak willpower. Once you sign up for the plan, the contributions just come off your paycheque automatically—you don't have to do a thing.

You don't have as many investment choices with a Group RRSP as you would with an individual RRSP; for instance, with a group plan, you might be limited to between ten and twenty-five options rather than thousands on your own. Some group plans also provide the employer match in the form of shares in the company. That might be a great investment, but it might not. And it concentrates your investments in shares of your employer and that can be risky. Still, the benefit of the company match far outweighs any of the downsides.

**EXERCISE**   ## Make the Most of Your Group RRSP Match

**RESEARCH:** Go to your company's intranet or ask your Human Resources contact to see if your company has a Group RRSP and how it works. Sometimes there is a waiting period before you can participate fully, for example. If you are already participating in the plan, find out how much you are contributing, what level of employer match you're getting, and what the maximum match level you're entitled to is. HR often runs workshops that focus on your Group RRSP or DCPP. Sometimes they even include snacks or lunch. Go to the workshop.

**INCREASE:** If you are getting anything less than the full employer match on your contribution, increase the amount you contribute to the Group RRSP. Do whatever it takes to find the money within your cash flow to maximize the match. If your employer offers a 100% contribution match, that means you are doubling your money. You contribute $1,000 and they contribute $1,000. Where else can you double your money without taking a crazy level of risk? You may also be able to increase your personal contribution even higher, so that you get as close to your 18% maximum RRSP contribution limit all in one place, and then you don't have to do anything else.

**TALK:** Bring up the Group RRSP at lunch with your colleagues and ask if they've heard of it and if they participate in it. Do it in a casual "did you see that crazy YouTube video?" kind of way, as I know well how taboo topics like this can be. In all likelihood your work friends don't fully understand how the employer match works, but they will be grateful to you for bringing it up. (It might take 40 years for them to write that thank-you note, but no matter.)

**What Happens to My Group RRSP When I Leave My Company?**

**QUESTION:**

*"I am soon going to quit my job to start my own business. I have about $40,000 in my Group RRSP. What happens to that money?"*

**ANSWER:**

The money is yours and you have a few options for what to do with it. Because it is a Group RRSP and not a Defined Contribution Pension Plan, your money is not "locked in." You can transfer it to an individual RRSP, or a Registered Retirement Income Fund (RRIF). Like an RRSP, money in a RRIF is sheltered but beginning at age 71 you are required to withdraw a certain amount each year and you can no longer make contributions. You could also buy an annuity with the proceeds from your Group RRSP or take the money out in cash. But this last option is a very bad idea unless you have some super special reason to do it—and don't tell me it is to fund your new business. You will pay income tax on that money, reducing the amount to a fraction of its former glory, and it won't be there for you when you retire. The annuity option might make sense if you are fairly close to retirement, but in all likelihood you should simply transfer it into an individual RRSP. You will then need to buy new investments with this money. The selection out there can be overwhelming, so you may want to refer to my first book, *Moolala*, for advice on how to choose low-cost investments that fit with your time frame till retirement.

Had you been enrolled in a Defined Contribution Pension Plan instead of a Group RRSP, you might have had the option to keep the money invested in your employer's plan, or you could have taken a lump sum and transferred it into a Locked-In Retirement Account, or LIRA. This type of RRSP still allows you to invest the money as you like, but there are restrictions on withdrawing it. Those restrictions vary by province, so it's best to find out how it will work for you. For quick access, I've put a link up on moolala.ca. Another aspect of a DCPP that is different than a Group RRSP is that to receive all the money, your employer's contribution must pass a "vesting period." This is the period of time that the employee must work at the company in order to fully own the employer contribution. If it hasn't vested you'll receive only the portion of your contribution that has vested.

~~~~~~~~~~~~~~~~~~~~~~~~~~~~~~~~~~~~~~~~~~~~~~~~~~~

**Spousal RRSPs: Sharing the wealth**

There are lots of marvellous reasons to find a life partner. Love, companionship, and of course, tax savings.

The spousal RRSP is a perk available to those who are married or in a common-law relationship. It allows a couple to split their retirement income more evenly, by shifting savings from the bigger bread-winner to the smaller one, so the same amount of retirement income is taxed at a lower rate. The income disparity might exist because one spouse has a higher-paying job than the other, or one doesn't work outside of the home. The bottom line is this: you will pay less tax on two incomes of $50,000 each than on one income of $100,000. While income splitting may not be the backbone of your relationship, it is a helpful way to reduce your family's overall tax bill.

Here are some other important things to know:

• **Your RRSP contribution limit is your limit:** If your personal contribution limit is $10,000, you can put part of that into your personal RRSP and part into your spousal RRSP—but no matter how you slice it you cannot contribute more than that amount. Said another way, you can contribute a total of $10,000, but you can choose to put some of that into your spouse's wine cellar and some of it into yours.

• **Your spouse's contribution limit remains theirs:** In other words, your spouse can continue to contribute to their own RRSP up to their own personal contribution limit.

- **The plan belongs to the spouse:** The assets in the spousal RRSP belong to the person whose name it is registered to and he or she is the one who makes the decisions on investments and withdrawing money from the plan. That said, a spousal RRSP is a different account from their personal RRSP and the CRA doesn't like it when you mix the two together.

- **Understand the attribution rule:** The three year attribution rule basically says that your contribution must stay in the plan for three years before it is withdrawn. This rule prevents the spouse from immediately withdrawing that money so it will be taxed at a lower rate. There are a few exceptions to the rule—during a marriage breakdown, for example.

Here's how it works: Let's say Evelyn earns more than her husband Gurpreet. During her career, she is able to contribute more to her RRSP than he can, saving up a larger nest egg. In retirement she withdraws $100,000 in income to support their lifestyle. Gurpreet is able to save less during his career, and so he withdraws less income in retirement, just $25,000 per year. The family tax bill based on their combined income is $28,750.

However, if Evelyn contributes some money to Gurpreet's spousal RRSP now, when they retire, his nest egg will be closer in size to hers, allowing him to withdraw more income in retirement than he otherwise would have been able to, and allowing her to withdraw less. She withdraws $75,000 and he withdraws $50,000, resulting in a family tax bill of $25,500, a savings of $3,250 each year. Imagine how fast the tax savings would add up over the twenty-five years of this couple's retirement.

## Comparing no spousal RRSP and spousal RRSP

|  | NO SPOUSAL RRSP | SPOUSAL RRSP | DIFFERENCE |
|---|---|---|---|
| **EVELYN** | | | |
| Annual retirement income | $100,000 | $75,000 | |
| Tax rate* | 26% | 22% | |
| Income tax payable | $26,000 | $16,500 | −$9,500 |
| **GURPREET** | | | |
| Annual retirement income | $25,000 | $50,000 | |
| Average tax rate | 11% | 18% | |
| Income tax payable | $2,750 | $9,000 | +$6,250 |
| **Total income tax per year** | **$28,750** | **$25,500** | **−$3,250** |

\*   Actual tax rates differ by province of residence. This example is for illustration only and uses the average tax rate on the retirement income.

This plan doesn't affect Evelyn's tax deduction or her contribution limit. And in addition to giving you tax savings, a spousal RRSP can also help you limit the OAS clawback that kicks in when your retirement income exceeds a certain amount.

There have been changes to pension splitting in the last few years that have negated some of the benefits of spousal RRSPs. But if you think you're going to be in a different tax bracket than your spouse in retirement, this strategy can make a difference.

I get asked an awful lot of questions about RRSPs, some of which we haven't covered yet. Skim through the Q&As below and read the ones that apply to you. Then do the exercise that has you actually choose a retirement savings vehicle.

---

**Q & A**    ## What Happens to Our Spousal RRSP If We Get a Divorce?

**QUESTION:**

*"I understand the benefits of a spousal RRSP but I'm also very practical. What happens to the money if my spouse and I get divorced?"*

**ANSWER:**

You love your spouse and your spouse loves you. But a pragmatist like you knows that marriage isn't always "Till death do us part," no matter how strong your intentions or how much work you do to keep the love alive. When it comes to spousal RRSPs I can provide a measure of comfort. While the spouse owns the plan and is the one who makes the decisions on it, generally speaking all assets are considered marital property. The house, gardening tools, and co-curated David Bowie LP collection have to be divvied up—amicably or not—and so do the investments.

Generally speaking, a divorce will involve a legal agreement that says, "Let's split the amount in the TFSA or RRSP 50/50" (or 40/60, or whatever split the parties involved have agreed upon in the context of the total assets). Once that agreement is complete, the amount in question can be transferred to the person one time only with no taxation. In most cases it's advised that, once both parties are satisfied, the transfer occurs quickly—generally within thirty days of the agreement's finalization.

If you had chosen not to use a spousal RRSP and instead contributed only to your own RRSP, you would still have to include those savings in  the marital property. So, all things being equal, you might as well contribute to a spousal RRSP while you're married and reap the tax benefits that result. Now, go give that spouse of yours some love and affection.

## Is It True What They Say About Death and Taxes?

**QUESTION:**

*"What happens to my RRSP if I die?"*

**ANSWER:**

It is going to happen to all of us sooner or later. Hopefully later. If you were to die, the money in your RRSP would be paid out to your beneficiary or to your estate. In general, the amount is included in the deceased person's final income tax return and is therefore taxed on the value of the plan before that payout occurs. This isn't surprising given that the RRSP was just deferring income tax, not eliminating it. But there are circumstances in which that tax can be deferred further—if the beneficiary is a spouse, a financially dependent child who is under age 18, or a financially dependent child of any age who is mentally or physically infirm.

If someone close to you dies you should consult a tax expert, since the scenarios and rules can be complex. However, there is one big action anyone can take now: name a beneficiary. This will minimize confusion and fees on probate and estate administration. And if you have been through a divorce, be sure to update your beneficiary. As amicable as your split might have been, it isn't that likely that you'll want them to have this money upon your death.

 ## Does Paying Down Debt Trump Saving in My RRSP?

**QUESTION:**

*"I am a 30-year-old single woman. I have a good job and am one of the lucky ones with a Defined Benefit Pension Plan. I purchased my first house about eighteen months ago. In addition to the mortgage and $5,000 loan from my RRSP under the Home Buyers' Plan,*

*I have $17,000 in student debt, a $7,000 car loan, and $9,000 in credit card debt. I do not have any difficulty making my payments. In fact, I regularly make additional payments on my car loan and credit card and I have also increased my student loan payment. I have about $2,500 in my RRSP and $1,500 in savings. Should I be contributing to my RRSP?"*

**ANSWER:**

You are not going to be single for long. Whether you happen to date men or women, you just need to find a way to work "financially responsible" into your online dating profile, alongside a reference to how much you "love *Hockey Night in Canada*."

Okay, the former might not improve your dating life and the latter might not be true, but you should definitely celebrate all the things that you are doing right when it comes to your money. You have a good job with a pension, you own your own home, and you're aggressively repaying your debt.

### The biggest bang for your buck

Now that you're done patting yourself on the back, we need to talk about priorities. Your approach to debt repayment is admirable, but scattered. Let's think through what you should be paying down first, so that you get the biggest bang for your buck. There are two principles to keep in mind:

1.  **Pay the minimums:** I wish this went without saying, but it doesn't. You always need to pay the minimum required by your loan agreement. Otherwise you will annoy the lender and take a hit on your credit score. But you should start by paying only the minimums, until you determine where to use your extra cash. What I mean is that you shouldn't be making extra payments on your car loan or student loan until you see if that math makes sense.

2.  **Pay the highest interest rate first:** The second principle is that you should pay down the debt that is costing you the most first. You aren't currently doing that. A car loan might have an interest

rate of 8% or so, your student loan 6% and your mortgage 3.5%. Compare those to a credit card that charges 20% interest. A $5,000 outstanding balance on your car loan costs you $400 in interest, your student loan, $300, and your mortgage, $175. That same amount outstanding on your credit card costs you $1,000! One. Thousand. Dollars. @!#*&!!

So you should do everything you can to pay off that credit card first and fast!

. . . . . . . . . . . . .

**You should do everything you can to pay off that credit card first and fast!**

. . . . . . . . . . . . .

### Reordering your debt priorities

Here is what you need to do to reorder your debt priorities:

- Organize your info: The first thing you need to do is write down your outstanding debts alongside the associated interest rates and minimum monthly payments. Here is an example using made-up numbers.

| DEBT | OUTSTANDING | INTEREST RATE | MINIMUM PAYMENT |
|------|-------------|---------------|-----------------|
| Credit card | $9,000 | 20% | $340 |
| Car loan | $7,000 | 8% | $300 |
| Student loan | $17,00 | 6% | $500 |
| Mortgage | $150,000 | 3.5% | $600 |
| Home Buyers | $5,000 | 0% | $50 |

- Set up automatic minimum monthly payments: You have already done this on your mortgage and likely your Home Buyers' Plan. But I'd consider taking your student loan payment back down to the minimum because its interest is likely at a way lower rate than your credit card.

- Focus every extra penny on your highest-rate debt: Now, instead of increasing your student loan or car loan payments, focus everything on eliminating your credit card debt. Once that is done, move on to the car loan, and on and on. Sometimes you aren't allowed to pre-pay too much—for example most mortgages have some restrictions on lump sum payments.

Hold off on RRSP contributions: Because you have a Defined Benefit Pension Plan, you can afford to hold off on RRSP contributions for now and focus on debt repayment instead. I know that was your actual question and I took forever and a day to answer it. Sorry about that, but worth it, right? If you didn't have a DBPP, I would recommend you have a similar approach to organizing your info. But I would also say you should contribute at least something to your RRSP to qualify for the tax deduction and get you into the habit of saving for retirement.

**My challenge to you**

Once you have your credit card paid off in full, my challenge to you is to never again hold an outstanding balance. Set up a line of credit secured against your home and use that in emergencies if you really need to, but pay off your credit card in full every month.

Promise?

### Should I Slash the Mortgage or Stock the Retirement Plan?

**QUESTION:**

*"When should I contribute extra cash to an RRSP versus to my mortgage?"*

**ANSWER:**

Math and mindset are both big factors in the choice between investing in an RRSP or paying down mortgage debt. While today's super low interest rates mean the math tilts towards contributing to your RRSP, there remains a lot of debate about which option is best. Here's my two cents, starting with the math.

### Math and the mortgage

Here is a simple example: If you take the extra money you have available and put it towards your mortgage you'll "earn" a guaranteed return equal to your mortgage rate, say 3.5%. If, instead, you put the money into your RRSP and invest it in the stock market through a low cost mutual fund or exchange-traded fund (more on these in chapter 12), your return over time could be around 6% based on long-term historical performance. You'll pay tax on that growth eventually, when you withdraw the money during retirement. Let's say you pay 30% in tax, the 6% return becomes 4.2% after tax. That 4.2% return on your RRSP is higher than the 3.5% cost on your mortgage repayment. The RRSP is the best choice based on the math, because 4.2% is higher than 3.5%. (Now, if you had been asking about RRSPs versus credit card debt, the answer would be different because that 4.2% on RRSPs would almost certainly be lower than the 20% to 25% interest you'd be paying on a card, making credit card debt the very first place you should put any free cash.)

If you choose your RRSP over your mortgage you'll also receive a larger tax refund right now that can either go towards additional debt repayment—including your mortgage—or right back into your RRSP, an especially powerful strategy if you're in a high tax bracket. Come on over to moolala.ca and check out the "mortgage versus RRSP calculator" there.

In most cases your income tax rate today is higher than it will be in retirement, so the RRSP offers better value than mortgage repayment because of the tax savings on the deduction. However, if you don't expect to be in a lower tax bracket in retirement—perhaps you have a generous pension coming to you—or you earn a modest income now, the mortgage repayment may make more sense.

The other point in favour of contributing to your RRSP instead of paying down your mortgage is diversification. For most Canadians, their house represents their biggest asset. RRSP contributions help diversify your investments so that you are not entirely reliant on the housing market.

Note that interest rates are at historic lows these days and as rates go up the math will shift in favour of mortgage repayment instead of RRSP contributions.

### Mindset and the mortgage

The math is one thing, but the mindset part counts too. A return of 6% on the stock market is by no means guaranteed, and the risk that investing entails might be too much for you. Plus, some people simply sleep better at night when they are plugging away at mortgage debt. That being said, other people feel more financially secure if they have savings for retirement or money that they can access in an emergency. You can withdraw money from an RRSP faster than pulling equity out of your home, although doing so will mean taking a tax hit.

There is also the challenge of remaining disciplined once your mortgage is paid off. If you are confident you'll invest your free cash in your retirement once you're mortgage-free, then put your extra cash towards the mortgage. However, if you aren't, put that extra cash into your RRSP so you can benefit from the "forced savings" that comes with a regular mortgage payment.

Good for you for seeing where your money can make the biggest difference to your future, instead of letting it slip through your fingers.

**EXERCISE** **Choose a Retirement Savings Vehicle**

Now it is time for you to choose a retirement savings vehicle. This choice is made based on your circumstances today and could change.

**REVIEW:** You basically have four options:

1.  **RRSP:** The Registered Retirement Savings Plan is the best option for most people, because of the tax deduction you'll receive and the tax-deferred growth on your investments.

2. **TFSA:** The Tax-Free Savings Account is best for people who expect to have a modest income for most of their working life, or who already have a Defined Benefit Pension Plan and won't see their income fall much after they stop working.

3. **Employer plan:** If you have a Group RRSP or a Defined Contribution Pension Plan at work you should probably choose this option to take advantage of the employer match.

4. **Combination:** Many of you will choose a combination of retirement savings vehicles. You might have a DBPP, Group RRSP or DCPP but want to top it up by saving in either an RRSP or a TFSA. Or you might take advantage of a spousal RRSP.

**CHOOSE:** Check the box to indicate your choice of retirement savings vehicles.

☐ RRSP

☐ TFSA

☐ Employer Plan: Group RRSP or Defined Contribution Pension Plan

☐ Combination (Check all that apply)
   ☐ RRSP
   ☐ TFSA
   ☐ Spousal RRSP
   ☐ Group RRSP
   ☐ Defined Contribution Pension Plan
   ☐ Defined Benefit Pension Plan

## Conclusion

A lot of people get stuck when choosing a retirement savings vehicle. Don't let that happen to you. Ponder the pros and cons above, make your choice, and then move on. Things are going to get a whole lot more interesting.

# { 9 }

## DETERMINE HOW MUCH
## YOU CAN CONTRIBUTE
### FIGURE OUT HOW MUCH YOU CAN
### AFFORD AND ARE ALLOWED

---

AT THIS point in the guide I hope that you are convinced of the importance of an RRSP, the metaphorical wine cellar for your retirement. You have articulated a retirement goal, and reviewed the various types of wine cellars to choose from. Now you need to determine how much you can contribute to the wine cellar you've got. The answer to this "how much" question is a function of two things: How much can you afford to contribute? And how much are you allowed to contribute?

### RRSP Contribution: What Is Affordable?

Despite the buzz out there at the start of RRSP season every February, the vast majority of Canadians simply can't afford to "max out" their RRSP contributions. As I mentioned earlier, only 24% of tax-filing Canadians contributed to an RRSP at all in 2011 and the average contribution was around $2,800, definitely under the maximum.

So, while there are always going to be people for whom socking away savings is as easy as making a Duncan Hines Swirl Cake, you can rest assured you're not the only one who can't afford to max out. The question of "how much can you contribute to your RRSP" will be determined more by what you can *afford* than what you are *allowed* to contribute.

The question of affordability is highly subjective. It comes down to the trade-offs that we make. Every day we trade off time, energy, and money, and for the most part we do this unconsciously. We'll talk more about how to become more mindful of trade-offs and how to increase what you can afford in chapter 10, but for now we need to find a starting point for your contributions.

### The Starting Point: 10% of your income

Many people look at the 18% maximum RRSP contribution limit and immediately shut down, unable to see how will it ever be possible for them to save that much. If that's you, I get where you're coming from.

I've been a runner for years. But I can't see how it will ever be possible for me to run fast enough to qualify for the Boston Marathon. It might be possible in theory, I don't know, but I'm not willing to do what it takes to try. The hard work and sacrifices are just more than I am up for.

The same might be true for you when it comes to maxing out your RRSP. Sure, it might be possible in theory to hit 18%, but it isn't going to happen in the real world, which is the one you live in.

> Sure, it might be possible in theory to hit 18%, but it isn't going to happen in the real world, which is the one you live in.

Instead of the 18% maximum, I would aim for 10% of your gross income, which is still a big number, I know. If you bring in $60,000 per year before taxes, you would aim to put $6,000 per year or $500 per month into your RRSP. Can you "afford" to take $500 out of your spending every month? Based on your current spending habits, perhaps not. But 10% is a starting point. And if you can't find a way to do 10%, then do 5%. That is much better than 0%. Remember, the most important thing is to get started.

**EXERCISE** **Apply the 10% Rule of Thumb**

**FIND:** Go to your pay stub from work and find out your gross income per year. This is the number before all the deductions that come off of your paycheque. If you are self-employed or have income that fluctuates month to month, use your gross income from last year as a proxy for what your income will be this year.

My gross income is: _____.

**CALCULATE:** Take your gross annual income and multiply it by 10% to find out what your annual RRSP contribution would be. Then divide that number by 12 to figure out what your monthly RRSP contribution would be.

My annual RRSP contribution would be: _____.

My monthly RRSP contribution would be: _____.

**COMPARE:** Compare this annual RRSP contribution number with what you *actually* contributed to your RRSP last year. Then check a box below.

☐ More: Actual RRSP contribution was more than 10% of income.

☐ Less: Actual RRSP contribution was less than 10% of income.

**Borrowing from the bank: Considering an RRSP loan**

Some of you might say that you can't afford to contribute anything to your RRSP. There is simply no extra money sitting around at RRSP time. If that describes your situation, it might make sense for you to take out an RRSP loan. The benefit of this strategy is that you will be able to contribute more to your RRSP and therefore qualify for a bigger tax refund to put towards debt repayment or a larger RRSP contribution. And repaying an RRSP loan can also act as a "forced savings" plan that can help keep you disciplined. This is especially true if your income fluctuates from month to month or year to year.

But the benefits of an RRSP loan come at a cost. You'll be paying interest on the loan, and that interest is not tax deductible. If the loan has an amortization of more than twelve months, the interest you'll pay will likely outweigh the tax benefit. Plus, the RRSP loan may gloss over the fact that you are simply living beyond your means and need to increase income or cut spending to allow you to save for retirement on an ongoing basis. If you have the cash to make a loan repayment, you have the cash to make an RRSP contribution. I'd lean towards simply making an RRSP contribution instead of signing up for a loan. That said, here is some background on your options.

1. **"Gross-up" RRSP loan:** With this type of loan, the bank will help you figure out how much your tax refund is likely to be, and then lend you money to increase your RRSP contribution so that the tax refund you receive will be enough to pay off the loan. Let's say, for example, that you're in the 30% tax bracket. You have $5,000 in the bank to make an RRSP contribution and you borrow an additional $2,000, bringing your total contribution to $7,000. At a 30% tax rate, that $7,000 will generate a $2,100 refund that will more than repay the $2,000 loan. In effect, the gross-up loan ensures that you contribute your tax refund to your RRSP instead of spending it on something you desperately want but don't desperately need. Like a Cannondale XC Full Suspension mountain bike or maybe even bi-annual Restylane filler treatments. (Don't worry. I won't tell a soul.)

2. **"Top-up" RRSP loan:** In this case you borrow from the bank to increase your RRSP contribution, and although the resulting tax refund is higher because you contributed more, it isn't enough to pay off the loan. Still, the amount you borrowed is manageable and you can pay it off within the year while also making this year's RRSP contribution. Remember that the interest you

pay on an RRSP loan is not tax deductible so if you can't pay it off within the year, you'd be better off just to set up an automatic withdrawal to your RRSP so that you'll get on track this year. This is a more sustainable strategy and doesn't leave you constantly playing catch up.

3. **"Catch-up" RRSP loan:** The third type of loan is designed so you can borrow a larger amount of money in an effort to use some of your excess contribution room from previous years. This loan will generate a larger tax refund, but you will still have to pay interest on it. This can make sense if you can afford to continue making regular RRSP contributions in addition to the loan, and if you do this once versus making it a habit. Instead of a catch-up loan, you can simply increase the amount you contribute to your RRSP every month and catch up interest-free over time, instead of in one potentially very expensive shot. I'd also recommend improving your cash flow so that you can increase your RRSP contribution every single month rather than borrowing to do it at the end of the tax year.

4. **Line of credit:** The last option is to borrow money for your RRSP contribution from an existing line of credit. The advantage to this approach is that it is super simple and you can pay the money back at your convenience. The disadvantage is also that you pay the money back at your convenience—because it might not be convenient for a while. I prefer the forced repayment plan that comes with a "gross-up" or "top-up" RRSP loan.

 ## What is the Financial Equivalent to Calling 9-1-1?

**QUESTION:**

*"I am struggling under a crushing debt load. I have a bunch of money in RRSPs and so far I haven't touched it. But I'm wondering if I should just cash everything in and put it towards my debt so I can stay afloat awhile longer."*

**ANSWER:**

You need to call a non-profit credit counsellor. Immediately. It sounds like you may be heading towards bankruptcy and you need a third party to take you through your options, which may include bankruptcy or something called a "consumer proposal."

Cashing in your RRSPs might get creditors off your back for now, but it also might just delay the inevitable and prolong your suffering. If you file for bankruptcy, for example, it is likely that you'll be able to keep your RRSP, thanks to changes made in 2008 to the Bankruptcy and Insolvency Act.

There are serious consequences to taking the bankruptcy path, but it might prove to be a better option for you because you'd be able to eliminate the debt, get a fresh start, and still hold on to something for your retirement.

Run, don't walk, to a computer and search for "Non-profit credit counselling" in your area. Do this now.

 **When it Comes to RRSPs, Can There Be Too Much of a Good Thing?**

**QUESTION:**

*"About 12 years or so ago, I read that I could overcontribute to my RRSPs by $2,000 dollars without any penalty and reap the benefits of having that extra money working away in my tax shelters. I had the money at the time so decided to try it. However, somehow an extra $2,000 was deposited to my RRSP. The CRA disapproved, let me know, and I withdrew the money using some special forms. Now, 10 years later, the over-contribution message is still on my notice of assessment every year. What, if anything, should I do?"*

**ANSWER:**

Your story is a cautionary tale for those who are considering using the RRSP over-contribution room as a strategy, instead of as a cushion. Sure, the strategy allows you to take advantage of a little bit of tax-deferred growth. But it was designed to simply protect you in case you contributed a little too much. And if you go over, the penalty is a hefty 1% per month on any amount that exceeds the $2,000 over-contribution limit.

The key point here is to watch your contribution limit and stay within it. You'll find it on the notice of assessment that Canada Revenue Agency sends you every year a few months after you file your tax return. As proud as you might feel about being one of the few who has been able to use up their allowable RRSP limit, you really don't want to have to pay the penalty tax.

You corrected your mistake pretty quickly by removing the funds, but for some reason the message is still on your file. I would call the CRA to find out why the message is still there, but more importantly to be 100% sure that you are not still being charged a penalty.

~~~~~~~~~~~~~~~~~~~~~~~~~~~~~~~~~~~~~~~~~~~

## RRSP Contribution: What Is Allowable?

I mentioned earlier that most people are constrained by how much they can *afford* to contribute to an RRSP. There are also limits on what you are *allowed* to contribute to your RRSP every year.

You can contribute an amount equal to 18% of your previous year's gross income, to a maximum contribution limit that goes up a little bit every year. The maximum contribution limit for 2013 is now just under $24,000. Say you made $70,000 last year, that'd be $12,600 you can put in the RRSP wine cellar this year.

For people who have rarely or never reached the RRSP contribution limit but whose fortunes have recently changed due to an inheritance, a bonus at work, or a lucrative patent on bottled sunshine, you'll be pleased to know that the contribution room is cumulative. This means that if you didn't max out in prior years, that room is still yours to take advantage of at a later date, when you can toss a nice, juicy lump sum into your RRSP to use up some of that contribution room you've been building over time.

**EXERCISE** | ### Determine How Much You Can Contribute

**FIND:** Dig through your papers and pull out the notice of assessment that the Canada Revenue Agency mailed to you after you filed your income taxes last year. It will tell you what your maximum RRSP contribution is, including your unused contribution room. If you can't find it, you can go to the CRA website, or give them a call, social insurance number in hand. Just be sure to have your Sudoku with you for the inevitable wait.

**WRITE:** Fill in the blanks below so you have all the info in one place.

RRSP deduction limit for _____ : ................. $ _____.

Your RRSP deduction limit for _____ : ................. $ _____.

You have: ....................................... $ _____

of unused RRSP contributions available for _____.

## Conclusion

You have now made significant progress on developing a simple plan for getting a handle on your retirement savings. You have articulated your retirement goal, chosen a retirement savings vehicle, and determined how much you can contribute to your RRSP. Step 3 is complete. And if I were there with you in person I'd raise a glass to celebrate your progress.

Now it's time to Zumba on over to Step 4, Take Action. This step will give you the skills you need to move outside your comfort zone, open up and contribute to your RRSP and determine what to invest your contribution in.

Maestro.

Music please.

# STEP 4

---

# TAKE ACTION

---

STEP 1
Lay the
foundation

STEP 2
Determine
how much
you need

STEP 3
Develop
the plan

STEP 4
Take
action

STEP 5
Stay
engaged

# { 10 }

## CONQUER YOUR COMFORT ZONE
### MAKE SURE YOU TAKE ACTION ON YOUR RETIREMENT SAVINGS PLAN

---

THE COMMUNITY centre near my house holds lots of different classes. One class in particular that piqued my interest was called "Zumba," which from my safe perch outside on the street looked like a cross between an '80s-era Jane Fonda aerobics class and Ricky Martin's wedding reception. I had been thinking about going to a class like this for months, but I was having a really hard time getting motivated. Think about your retirement savings for a minute. Sound familiar?

When it comes to getting a handle on your RRSP, it isn't always easy to follow through and take action on the plan. But now that you have determined what you want and developed a plan to get it, the next step is to take action. Step 4 of the Moolala Method focuses on moving that plan from your notebook (or napkin) into your real life. In a few minutes we'll get to the part of your plan where you actually contribute to an RRSP. But before we do that I want to address why it can be so bloody hard to take action.

### Identifying the Hurdles to Taking Action

It is hard to take action, but my hurdle might be different from yours, given that there are so many to choose from: complacency, laziness, other spending priorities like debt repayment or the mortgage, or a lack of interest in or knowledge of retirement savings. I asked members of the Moolala Community what hurdles prevented them from taking action on their retirement savings.

*"Boredom. My eyes just glaze over and I can't concentrate when the topic comes up. I know I should work on this, but I can't maintain the interest."*
—Sandra, 36, sales rep. Single.

*"Time. I have three young kids. I have so little time to do anything other than manage the chaos around me."*
—James, 45, contractor. Married with three kids.

*"Volatile income. I'm self-employed so I never know how much I'll earn in a year."*
—Andrea, 42, consultant. Married with two kids.

*"Divorce. I went through a separation and bankruptcy, then divorce. It was hard enough to stretch the dollars to cover day-to-day living, and retirement savings were very last on the list for a long time."*
—Cynthia, 50, journalist. Divorced with two adult children.

*"Discipline. Lattes today are more important to me than food in thirty years."*
—Carolyn, 43, HR consultant. Married with one child.

*"Trust. When it comes to my advisor my trust is so low. I've had so little attention I find it hard to imagine someone even wanting to work with my situation."*
—Karleen, 51, small business owner. Married.

*"My husband. I can't seem to inspire my husband to save money. He has debts at high rates of interest and needs to pay those off first. There's always one in every family, right?"*
—Farah, 42, software developer. Married with two kids.

If you read between the lines of these answers, there is one common theme—one fundamental hurdle that makes it so hard to take action on your retirement savings. It's the same hurdle that made it so hard for me to walk into that Zumba class.

Fear.

In my case it was a fear of looking stupid in front of other people. In your case it could be a fear of confronting the sorry state of your retirement savings, not being able to "keep up with the Joneses," or the sacrifices you may have to make to get back on track. It could be the fear of getting old, or the fear of looking stupid in front of other people, such as your financial advisor, your spouse, or your family.

Fear is at the root of procrastination, and that may be what is going on with you. But rather than try to process your fear, hide it, or overcome it, I would recommend you simply acknowledge that you will likely be fearful as you move outside of your comfort zone. 'Twas ever thus. That way you won't sit there waiting for the fear and boredom to dissipate, or the discipline and time to magically appear. It probably won't, so you may as well not waste your time.

 **EXERCISE**   ## Identify Your Hurdle to Taking Action

**PONDER:** Review some of the examples from the Moolala Community and ponder what *your* primary hurdle is when it comes to taking action on your retirement savings.

**WRITE:** Now jot your answer down. It may not be the definitive answer, but it is your answer for now.

My main hurdle to taking action on my retirement savings is

_____.

I'll give you an opportunity to identify actions you could take to overcome this hurdle at the end of the chapter. For now, just let the hurdle marinate itself in the fridge for a bit.

## Moving Outside Your Comfort Zone: What Will It Take for You to Take Action?

I finally found the courage to show up at the Zumba class. Janet, the instructor, was fun, friendly, and totally rocked the routine. So did most of the exuberant, lululemon-clad women busting out their best moves to samba and salsa. And then there was me: the only dude in the room. But I was there, wasn't I? And that was a victory in itself.

As you worked your way through this guide I asked you to think a bit about what want for yourself and your family in retirement. Then you developed a plan for your retirement savings. Now is the time to actually *take* action on that plan.

I know, easier said than done, right? In my experience, "what it takes" is a combination of courage, creativity, patience, and discipline.

**COURAGE:** Moving outside your comfort zone to take action on your retirement savings can prompt a certain level of fear. It will take courage to overcome that fear and change your habits—to say no to your spouse, your kids or yourself and take action anyway.

**CREATIVITY:** For some people, hurdles will present themselves that require creativity to overcome. For example, you may have to figure out different ways to increase income or cut spending, or be creative in finding the time to visit the bank without having to deal with your three-year-old's tantrums at the branch.

**PATIENCE:** Saving for a vacation in six months takes a certain level of patience, but nowhere near what it might take for you to save for retirement twenty, thirty or forty years down the road. I don't have a lot of patience to begin with, and much of it gets used up dealing with traffic, call centres, and a child who complains that her big girl bed is both "too big and too small."

**DISCIPLINE:** I would rather watch *The Amazing Race* than work on my retirement savings, and I'm sure you have other things that you would prefer to do too. To take action on your retirement savings plan you will likely need to do things that you don't particularly want to do. It will take discipline to keep moving forward when you're disinterested, defeated, tired, or tempted by other things.

So let's get personal and look at what it is going to take for you to take action.

 **EXERCISE**   ## Identify What It Will Take for You to Take Action

**PONDER:** As we discussed in chapter 3, you probably have certain behaviours in the area of money that don't work so well for you. Think about some of those behaviours, and then ask yourself what it is going to take for you to take action on your retirement savings.

- Where will you need courage?

- Where will you need to be creative?

- Where will you need to be patient?

- What will you need to be disciplined about?

- What else is it going to take for you to take action on your plan?

_____

_____

**ASK:** Now that you have a sense of what it is going to take, ask yourself this question: "Am I willing to *do* what it takes?"

☐  **Yes:** If your answer is yes, good for you. Later in the guide, in Step 5 of the Moolala Method, I'll give you some ideas on how to stay engaged with your plan over time.

☐ **No:** If your answer is no, thanks for being honest. No is a valid answer, and answering that way doesn't make you a bad person. In fact, being honest with yourself might ease some of the anxiety you have about your financial situation. There will be consequences associated with not taking action, but they might be consequences you're willing to deal with.

☐ **Not sure:** If you're not sure you're willing to do what it takes, ask yourself this supplementary question, "What will it take for me to be sure in my answer?" See what pops into your head. Sitting on the fence is natural. But stay there too long and the chain-link can really start biting into your skin.

**TALK:** As I explained in *Moolala*, one of the best things you can do when it comes to taking action on your money is to talk about your plan with a few of your friends and family. They can provide you with the support, ideas, and accountability that will make all the difference in you getting what you want for your retirement. So go out there and talk.

## Conclusion

If you take no actions, it is pretty much guaranteed that you will get no results. The result we're focused on is you getting a handle on your retirement savings, so let's move on to the next set of skills for you to master: how to open up an RRSP and then how contribute to it. If you haven't done these things before they might seem like daunting tasks, but they really aren't hard in practice. If you already have an RRSP, skim ahead to the part where I talk about determining what to invest your contribution in.

# { 11 }

## OPEN UP AN RRSP AND CONTRIBUTE TO IT

### GRAB YOUR ID AND GO
### SIGN THE FORM

---

**A**N RRSP wine cellar can be yours for free or nearly free, thanks to your friendly neighbourhood financial institution. It is as simple to open as a bank account and you can complete much of the process online. Or you can get dressed, brush your teeth and get your smart self to the bank or credit union in person. Bring government ID, your social insurance number, and your sense of humour. When you arrive simply say to the receptionist, "I'd like to open an RRSP." Sit down on a cushy chair, say yes to the free cup of coffee or tea, and wait for the account manager to call you into his or her office.

## Opening a New Account . . . or Accounts

Whether you open your RRSP online or in person, you will be asked what type of RRSP you would like to set up—a basic or individual RRSP, or a self-directed RRSP.

### Basic or Individual RRSP

A basic or individual RRSP is designed to hold only certain types of investments, such as GICs, mutual funds, or even cash. You can open this type of RRSP with a bank, credit union, or mutual fund company. The bank representative or financial advisor will likely sell you mutual funds and you'll get some financial advice along with the transaction.

There is something called an "RRSP savings account" and I don't recommend opening one. This option is like a traditional savings account and you can only hold cash in it. With interest rates as low as your average politician's approval rating you won't get much of a return.

If your RRSP contains less than $25,000 and the thought of learning much more about investing makes you want to cry, keep your complexity low and open up a basic RRSP. If, however, your assets are above that level and you can see yourself getting more engaged with your money—even looking at different investing options—a self-directed RRSP might make more sense.

## Self-directed RRSP

A self-directed RRSP is one that can hold almost any type of investment—mutual funds, exchange-traded funds, stocks, bonds, you name it. You can open this type of RRSP at a brokerage—either a full-service brokerage or a discount brokerage. The big banks generally have a full-service brokerage option available for clients with more than $200,000 to invest, and a discount brokerage open to everyone. The former includes the services of a financial advisor, for which you will pay either a commission or a fee based on your total assets, and the latter offers no advice, but provides trading services for the cost of a movie ticket.

As with bank accounts, there is no limit to the number of RRSP accounts you can open. But for simplicity it makes sense to have as few accounts as possible.

Setting up a spousal RRSP is just as simple as setting up one for yourself, and in fact you might want to do it at the same time. Enrolling in a Group RRSP or a Defined Contribution Pension plan doesn't involve your bank. Instead you'll talk to your company's HR department.

## Contribute to an RRSP:
## Get Some Money into Your Account

Once you have opened the RRSP or gotten yourself the wine cellar, it is time to put something into it. In chapter 9 you figured out how much you can contribute, either based on what you can afford or what you are allowed. Now you just have to contribute that money to your RRSP. The friendly representatives at your financial institution will help you with the logistics, and they can generally link your RRSP account to your other bank accounts so that you can make transfers online in the future. I also recommend that you set up a pre-authorized contribution so that you don't have to think about your RRSP every February—an idea I'll talk more about in chapter 14.

### Beat the clock: Contribute before the end of February deadline

Everyone gets so breathless about the RRSP contribution deadline, which is usually March 1, except in a leap year or when that date falls on a Sunday. In both those instances the RRSP deadline is the last day of February. You just have to get the money in by then. You can choose what you want to invest that money in at a later date.

Ideally you want to make your contribution before the deadline so you'll get the tax deduction this year. But what happens if you miss the deadline? Nothing really. You won't be able to claim the tax deduction this year, so you won't get as big a refund. But remember that your contribution room is cumulative, so whatever you don't use this year will be carried forward to next year, meaning you can claim the deduction next year instead. Now you're ahead of the game.

> Ideally you want to make your contribution before the deadline so you'll get the tax deduction this year.

**EXERCISE**    ## Open Up an RRSP and Contribute To It

This was the shortest exercise for me to type, but it might not be the shortest for you to complete. Block off some time in your calendar to do these two things.

**OPEN:** Book an appointment at your bank or credit union to open up an RRSP.

**CONTRIBUTE:** Transfer some money in. At this stage, I'll be happy even if it's only $10 because then at least you'll have an RRSP and you'll have something inside it.

## Conclusion

Many of you breezed through this chapter because you already have an RRSP set up, and good for you. For those of you who went out and signed up for one, good for you too. Now let's take a look at your options for what to invest your money in.

# { 12 }

## DETERMINE WHAT TO INVEST YOUR CONTRIBUTION IN
### DIVERSIFY YOUR RETIREMENT SAVINGS

---

**A** WINE CELLAR *holds* wine. But it isn't wine itself. An RRSP *holds* investments but is not an investment itself. So now that you have contributed money into your RRSP you need to determine what to invest that contribution in.

In all likelihood you don't have the time right now for a lot of detail on this topic. I'll outline the basics here and recommend that you take a look at *Moolala: Why Smart People Do Dumb Things with Their Money (and What You Can Do About It)*, in which I cover investing extensively.

### Delighting in Diversification

---

Your RRSP should have a few different types of investments inside of it to give you what is called "diversification." This is the idea that you should spread out your risk, rather than putting all of your eggs in one basket, as it were. It will matter less if some of your investments do poorly for a few years if you are diversified because your other investments may have performed better during the same time period.

## Mutual Funds Are an Easy First Step

If you are just starting to save for retirement, the investment product you will be offered most frequently is a mutual fund. A mutual fund pools together money from thousands of people, then the fund manager uses that money to buy stocks or bonds that they believe will perform well. If you already have some retirement savings and aren't sure if you have mutual funds, pull out one of your old statements and look up a few of the products that are included on it to see what you've got.

Holding one single mutual fund will provide you with some diversification because the manager of the fund will buy stock in many different companies. But you will also want to diversify across regions, having investments in the United States and internationally in addition to Canada.

### More than Baskin Robbins:
### Understanding the different kinds of mutual funds

Baskin Robbins has 31 different flavours of ice cream. When I was a kid that seemed an infinite selection—one I couldn't imagine ever working my way through in a lifetime of licking, especially given my loyalty to rocky road. Investing your retirement savings would be much simpler if there were just 31 mutual funds for people to choose from. However, there are over three thousand mutual funds in the freezer, so I wanted to take a few minutes to cover the basic types you'll find. I won't be making any recommendations on which funds to buy, because the selection changes so often and because it is important to choose funds that best fit your individual circumstances.

### Equity Mutual Funds: Buying a teeny tiny piece of Google

When you buy an "equity mutual fund" you are buying a fund that holds "equity" or stocks. That mutual fund manager is buying tiny pieces of companies, in the form of shares in those companies, on the belief that those shares will be worth more in the future than they are today.

Your equity mutual fund could focus on a number of different areas. For example, the fund could focus on companies located in Canada, the United States, Europe, or in the so-called emerging markets around the world. It could also focus on a type of company—ones that are positioned for growth, for example—or on a particular industry such as technology or financial services. The type of fund is usually captured in its name. "ACME U.S. Equity Fund" indicates that the fund manager is buying shares in American companies.

There are a lot of very specialized mutual funds out there. But I prefer choosing four to six funds that give you solid diversification, rather than trying to figure out which niche sectors are going to shoot the lights out.

### Fixed-income or bond mutual funds: Loaning your money out

Instead of using your money to buy a tiny piece of a company, when you buy a fixed-income mutual fund you are loaning your money to a corporation or to a government in the form of a bond. The interest the borrower gives you on that bond is your "fixed income," meaning that the interest income you receive doesn't fluctuate. So, when you buy into a fixed-income mutual fund, often referred to as a bond fund, you're loaning money to, say, the Canadian government so that they can build a bridge. The government then gives you a guaranteed 4% return on your loan. Isn't that nice?

As this example suggests, the *point* of buying fixed income is not so much about increasing value but about holding the current value of your investment and providing you with some stable income. You want to have some of both so that you're diversified—there is that word again. When equity is on a roll, the performance of bonds will likely be lacklustre by comparison. And when equity is a dog's breakfast, you'll be very glad to have the stable return of fixed income. There is a trade-off between risk and return. Super safe investments generally deliver lower returns; riskier ones have the potential for higher returns. While super safe investments might fit your personality best, it is important to take some risk so your investments will at least keep up with inflation.

### Balanced mutual funds: A mix of equity and fixed income

The third broad category of mutual funds is called "Balanced Mutual Funds." These funds bring together equity and fixed income into one fund, allowing you to have the growth potential of equity and the stability of fixed income in one place.

 **What the Heck Is an Exchange-Traded Fund? And Why Should I Care?**

**QUESTION:**

*"I have been reading the financial pages more over the last few months and have been seeing the term "exchange-traded funds" a lot. What does it mean and should I be considering investing in this type of product?"*

**ANSWER:**

Exchange-traded funds, or ETFs, are getting a lot of attention because they provide the diversification of a mutual fund at a much lower cost. There is no fund manager actively trying to determine which stocks will go up and which will go down. Instead the ETF passively mirrors the performance of an index, for example the TSX Composite or the S&P 500.

The main advantage of an ETF is cost. The product is cheaper to hold than a mutual fund, and that can mean it performs better for you. However, an ETF is a little more complex to buy. If you aren't working with a financial advisor at a full-service brokerage, you'll need to have a self-directed RRSP account at a discount broker in order to purchase them. You also don't get financial advice at a discount brokerage. Mutual funds, on the other hand, generally include a commission to the person who sold them to you, who will provide advice on an ongoing basis. And if you are buying ETFs in small quantities the trading commissions can be prohibitive.

## How Much of Each Type of Fund

You've contributed money into your RRSP and you now understand that you'll want to have some equity in your portfolio and some fixed income. But how much should you have of each? I'll outline two simple rules of thumb below, but if you are working with a financial advisor they will factor in other variables. Your marital status, the assets of your spouse, or availability of a Defined Benefit Pension may justify a different approach.

### Rule of thumb #1: Fixed income = your age

The amount of fixed income you have in your retirement savings should be about equal to your age.

For example, if you're 40 years old, about 40% of your total portfolio should be in fixed income. If you have $50,000 saved for retirement, about $20,000 of that amount should be in fixed income and the remaining $30,000 in equity.

Here's why: the younger you are, the more risk you can afford to take, because if the stock market falls, there is time for even your equity-heavy portfolio to rebound. But as you get older you'll want less risk that means more fixed income and less equity—because you'll need access to the money sooner, relying more on the *income* in the phrase *fixed income*. In short, you'll be less concerned about your portfolio growing and more concerned with it holding its value and spinning off income to cover your groceries and activities in retirement.

So you may be wondering, why not wait until you actually retire to buy any fixed-income mutual funds? Because if you hold only equities, you will be hit harder when the stock market inevitably dips, as it did in 2008. It's all about diversification. Age-appropriate diversification, that is.

> **EXERCISE**    **Apply the Fixed-Income Rule of Thumb**
>
> **WRITE:** Fill in the blanks below.
>
> I am _____ years old. Therefore about _____%
> of my retirement savings should be in fixed income.

### Rule of thumb #2: Equity divided into three equal parts

The amount remaining in your portfolio is then divided equally amongst three types of equity—Canadian, U.S. and International. The rationale, again, is diversification.

For example, if 40% of your money is in fixed income, the remaining 60% of your funds should go into equities according to an equal split: 20% Canadian equity, 20% U.S. equity and 20% international equity. (If you can't make an entirely equal split, as in some cases in the table below, just round up or down—remember, I like to keep things simple.)

### How much of each type: An example

|                      | AGE 30 | AGE 40 | AGE 50 | AGE 60 |
|----------------------|--------|--------|--------|--------|
| Fixed income         | 30%    | 40%    | 50%    | 60%    |
| Canadian equity      | 23%    | 20%    | 17%    | 13%    |
| US equity            | 23%    | 20%    | 17%    | 13%    |
| International equity | 23%    | 20%    | 17%    | 13%    |

The person selling you the investments for your RRSP will be able to give you more insight into other variables to consider. But, as you'll recall, I'm a big fan of low complexity. If you're 40 years old and have $50,000 saved, based on these two rules of thumb, your portfolio would look like this.

**How much: A 40-year-old with $50,000**

|  | AGE 40 | PORTFOLIO TOTAL |
|---|---|---|
| Fixed income | 40% | $20,000 |
| Canadian equity | 20% | $10,000 |
| U.S. equity | 20% | $10,000 |
| International equity | 20% | $10,000 |

 ## Should I Have More Mutual Funds Than Pairs of Shoes?

**QUESTION:**

*"I have been contributing to my RRSP for about fifteen years. I pulled out my most recent mutual fund statement and counted sixteen different mutual funds in my account. Why do I have so many and do I need them all?"*

**ANSWER:**

Mutual funds should not follow the principles of haute couture. Yet you have opened up your statement only to find that you have funds that were once the talk of the fall collection in Paris but didn't stand the test of time. Why do you have so many funds? Probably because they were in "fashion" during RRSP season one year and you bought into the latest trend. Marketing mutual funds is a very competitive business, and in any given year certain funds get lots of attention, thanks to heavy advertising, promotion, and sales incentives for financial advisers.

Now to the question of whether you need them all. My answer is no. A well-diversified portfolio can be created with four to six mutual funds at most. If you have more than that, your portfolio can grow too complex and unwieldy.

My recommendation to you is to look at the performance of your mutual funds over the long term, at least five years. Then go back to the place where you bought them and ask for some help to simplify things. Be particularly careful not to trigger any additional com-missions—called deferred sales charges, or DSCs—when you sell out, as you don't want to take that hit. And in future, instead of buy-ing into the latest fad, invest more in the basic, boring mutual funds that provide you the diversification you need at a low cost.

 **The Financial Headlines Scare Me. Can You Please Talk Me off the Ledge?**

**QUESTION:**

*"I have to confess to leaving most of my portfolio in cash. With the markets so crazy and Europe so scary, I have been afraid to do anything. My initial plan was to have 60% in fixed income—now that I'm 60—and 40% in equity. Is that still a good idea? I definitely need a pep talk."*

**ANSWER:**

I think you need to cancel your newspaper and perhaps your cable TV too. You are right that the markets are crazy and Europe is scary. But what is even crazier is you leaving your portfolio in cash. Less news might be just what you need to get yourself back on track. Here are a few points to ponder:

1. **Fear sells:** You may have heard the expression "If it bleeds, it leads." That's a reference to how the media often prioritizes stories. That's not to say that stock market gyrations and the European financial crisis aren't real or relevant. They are both. But over the long term—and retirement savings are held over the long term—the stock market has done very well. Your fear has you behaving in a less than rational way.

2. **Inflation eats cash:** Prices rise over time. As we reviewed in chapter 5, the cost of a cup of coffee next year will be more than it is today. Over the long term, inflation will clock in at about 2% a year, which means that your money needs to increase in value by at least 2% per year just to keep up. If it doesn't, you lose purchasing power. In other words, that cup of coffee gradually becomes harder and harder to afford, which is not good as you head into retirement. Sure, you might be a very conservative investor, but you need to factor in not only stock market risk, but also inflation risk. And then take rational steps to avoid it.

3. **Fixed income is different from equity:** You are leaving most of your money in cash when really your fears are mostly linked to the equity portion of your portfolio. (Said another way, you're throwing the proverbial baby out with the bath water.) Fixed income and equity don't behave in the same way. In fact, the reason you should hold both is to diversify your risk. If you are concerned about the stock market, then what you're really concerned about are your equity holdings; there is no reason not to hold fixed-income vehicles such as government bonds, GICs, a bond ETF, or a low-cost bond mutual fund. Use the basic rule of thumb on how much fixed income to hold—an amount approximately equal to your age. To answer your question, yes, I still think that basic asset allocation is a good idea.

4. **Timing the market is virtually impossible:** I was going to say that timing the market was impossible, but I decided to add "virtually" to silence the howls of protest that would accompany such an unequivocal remark. Your decision to hold cash is basically an attempt to time the market, or in other words, to figure out when to put your money back in for maximum gain. The data against this strategy is pretty compelling—even among professional money managers—so I wouldn't recommend trying it yourself.

5. **You still have some time for your investments to recover:** It may not feel like you have time, given that you're just five years away from when many people retire. But you do. After you retire you'll

rely on your investments to supplement any other income you have, such as CPP, OAS, or a pension. Your fixed-income investments will provide income, of course, and you'll start selling off your equities bit by bit. But you won't be selling them all on the day you turn 65 years old. Some you'll hold onto for many more years, and so there is time for them to rebound in value.

As for your request for a pep talk: put your money back to work for you in low-cost vehicles that give you a balance between capital appreciation and preservation. Said another way, "Keep calm and carry on."

---

**EXERCISE**   **Do Just One Thing**

We have covered a lot of ground—and you're still here. Hooray for you. As we wrap up Step 4: Take Action, I want you to put the guide down for a minute and go out and do just that: take action.

**CHOOSE:** Skim through the list of actions that we have covered so far and choose one that you could take action on right now. I want you to have the experience of accomplishment that taking action provides.

It doesn't have to be a big action—it could be as simple as calling your bank and booking an appointment to talk to someone, or going through your papers and finding your notice of assessment from Canada Revenue Agency. Or it could be an action that would address one of the hurdles you identified at the beginning of Step 4. If your hurdle to taking action is time, for example, you could book a babysitter for next Sunday to give you a full day to get on top of this.

**DO:** Now, just do it.

## Conclusion

Taking action on your retirement savings will help you get what you want in life. I know it might require something on your part: creativity, patience, discipline, courage, or whatever it is for you. But you *do* have what it takes. It may not feel like it sometimes, but you really do. Remember that no actions will deliver no results, but even the tiniest action, the smallest step forward, can get your momentum going.

Step 4 of the Moolala Method was about taking action—to open up an RRSP, contribute something to it, and determine where to invest that contribution. The next and final step is about how to Stay Engaged with the plan you have now set in motion. One of the best ways to do that is to make retirement savings a habit that is simply a part of your life.

# STEP 5

---

# STAY ENGAGED

---

# { 13 }

## MAKE IT STICK
### DEVELOP SOLID HABITS AROUND
### RETIREMENT SAVINGS

---

THE DENTAL hygienist was getting more insistent with every visit. Her periodic prodding about the importance of flossing my teeth had started with a gentle suggestion and was now a dire warning. I needed to start flossing regularly or face the very real consequences of [insert ominous music]... gum disease.

It wasn't that I objected to flossing on religious or political grounds. I knew how to do it. The process itself was a skill I had learned in childhood and was only a minor annoyance. I even be lieved her when she said it was in my best interests. The issue was, quite simply, that I had never developed the habit of flossing my teeth.

As I mentioned at the beginning of this guide, getting a handle on your retirement savings is a function of three things—knowledge, skills and habits. Having read this far, you have picked up a lot of new knowledge. And we've worked on some skills required to execute a plan to achieve your retirement goals. Now is the time to focus on developing good habits around retirement savings. Why? Because improving those habits is the easiest way to stay engaged with your plan.

Step 5 is perhaps the most crucial step of all because it is the one that will affect your retirement savings the most over time. If you stop short of Step 5—that is, you Take Action but don't Stay

Engaged—you'll have a nice one-time bump in your retirement savings but nothing sustainable. And what a missed opportunity that would be.

## Retirement Savings Is a Habit

A habit is a pattern of behaviour that we acquire. We follow that pattern again and again until it becomes almost involuntary. Most of us have good habits in some areas of life, and not-so-good habits in other areas. Think about your own habits around eating, exercising, sleeping, socializing, cleaning, smoking, flossing, and yes, retirement savings.

**Getting a handle on your retirement savings is a function of three things—knowledge, skills and habits.**

In chapter 3 of this guide, we talked about some of the behaviours that you could classify as either strengths or weaknesses. You could say that those behaviours are habits and they are either "good" or "bad." Now, when I say good or bad, I don't mean that you're a good or bad person. Bad habits will not send you on an express train to hell. And good habits will not earn you a membership at the health club in heaven. When it comes to your retirement savings, good habits are simply more likely to get you what you want than bad habits.

Here are some examples of habits, both good and bad:

## Money behaviours: Assessing your habits

| BEHAVIOUR | BAD HABIT | GOOD HABIT |
| --- | --- | --- |
| Knowledge | Not tracking your progress towards building your retirement nest egg | Knowing what you need to save to retire and tracking your progress |
| Spending | Buying things unconsciously | Making conscious choices about spending money |
| Saving | Not saving money consistently | Saving money consistently, even automating the process so you don't have to think about it |
| Tax vehicles | Racing to beat the RRSP deadline and often under-contributing, if you contribute at all | Contributing to your RRSP every month of every year |
| Investment performance | Being oblivious to how your investments are performing | Being aware of how your investments are performing |
| Organization | Leaving papers in disarray | Having a simple system for what goes where and what needs to happen when |
| Communication | Avoiding the topic of retirement savings with your spouse, family, and financial advisor | Engaging in periodic conversations about retirement savings with your spouse, family, and financial advisor |
| Taking action | Procrastinating when it comes to retirement savings | Following through on a basic retirement savings plan<br><br>Flipping through the *Moolala RRSP Guide to Rockin' Your RRSP* once per year |

I eventually came to realize that if I was going to change my bad habit of not flossing, I was going to need to do more than just think about it. I needed a plan. A very simple plan, mind you. This was only about flossing, not a crack addiction.

First, I bought a new super slick dental floss that was easy to use. And second, I put a recurring note in my calendar for Monday, Wednesday, and Friday of every week. (I mean, who wants to floss on weekends?). I would see that recurring appointment in my calendar and more often than not begrudgingly pull out the dental floss and get it done. After about a month or so I could confidently say that I had ingrained the habit. When it comes to your retirement savings, which good habits would make the biggest difference for you? Here are some examples of new good habits from the Moolala Community:

- **Meeting with a financial advisor**
  *"The change I made was to put a note about meeting with my financial advisor in my calendar. Now I remember to book it. He updates my retirement nest egg number and gives me an idea of how I have been progressing."*
  —Candice, 46, store manager. Married with two kids.

- **Having a family check-in**
  *"Now that I'm married, the conversation I used to have with myself is a joint conversation, and that took some getting used to. But we just kept at it and got better about discussing hot-button issues in a loving, adult fashion. I put it into the family calendar so we remember to talk about it once every three months. Sometimes it is just five minutes and other times it is three hours as we go through our investments."*
  —Joyce, 38, teacher. Married with one child.

- **Stop worrying**
  *"I got out of the habit of worrying about my money so much. Doing the nest egg exercise helped, as did some anxiety strategies I got from a great self-help book. This included reframing*

*my thinking about* RRSPS *as a necessity in life, like grocery shopping, instead of a daunting task to be avoided."*

—Angie, 46, administrative assistant. Divorced with two kids.

- **Take time to decide on purchases**
  *"I became self-employed and could no longer rely on a consistent income. That has been an incredibly humbling and valuable experience, because now I think long and hard before making spontaneous purchases (well, most of the time!). I find that by waiting and thinking things through I make smarter decisions and I usually conclude that I don't need whatever it is in the first place. This has freed up the cash to contribute to retirement savings."*

  —Jason, 42, IT consultant. Married with one child.

- **Simplify my habits**
  *"I stopped trying to track my spending. It was just taking too much time. Instead I stopped using my credit card and limited the amount of cash I have in my wallet. This worked for me."*

  —Nisha, 35, finance manager. Single.

**Tips for Changing Habits**

Habits are deeply ingrained, which is why it can be so difficult to change them, in any area of life. Here are a few ideas on how to foster good habits when it comes to retirement savings:

- **Change the physical:** Do something to change your physical environment so you won't have to rely only on your brain to change the habit. You could also say this is changing the "trigger." Instead of hoping I would remember to floss, I cleared away everything on a shelf of my medicine cabinet except dental floss and my toothbrush. That provided a prominent physical reminder, or trigger, that was very helpful. When it comes to improving your retirement savings habits, you could take your credit card out of your wallet and put it in the freezer; you could buy a fantastic lunch bag and store leftovers on the top shelf of the fridge where you can see them; you could book a coffee date with a friend beside your bank and meet her there after you've met with your financial advisor.

- **Keep tasks small:** It can be daunting to think about the big task of getting a handle on your retirement savings. Instead, think small and choose specific tasks you can do regularly so you don't get overwhelmed.

- **Choose only a few habits:** Don't try to work on everything at once. Be selective and choose one or two habits to work on at a time. Once they are ingrained, you can expand your focus to include other new, good habits.

- **Make the most of mornings:** Your willpower is usually strongest in the morning, because it hasn't yet been worn down by the demands of the day. Take action to develop good habits in the morning, when it is easier for your psyche.

- **Connect good habits to a reward:** It would defeat the purpose to connect your good retirement savings habit to a big financial reward. However, you want your brain to remember this behaviour in the future and a reward is a good way to do that. Perhaps after your monthly money meeting you and your spouse go out to a trashy Hollywood RomCom. Or perhaps your reward is as simple as crossing the action off a list prominently displayed on your fridge.

- **Take a metaphorical quaalude:** It generally takes thirty days of practise to change a habit. That is a long time, and inevitably you'll have some successes and some failures along the way. Be patient. Remember that once this habit is ingrained you won't even think of it as a habit—it will just be the way you do things.

- **Don't "try," says Yoda:** The phrase "I'll try" is a cop-out, at least according to *Star Wars: The Empire Strikes Back*. Yoda had some pointed and practical advice for Luke Skywalker.

LUKE. All right, I'll give it a try.

YODA. No. Try not. Do... or do not. There is no try.

Instead of "trying," take a few small actions that will help you change the way you behave when it comes to your retirement savings.

**EXERCISE**  **Improve Your "Good" Habits One at a Time**

**REVIEW:** Skim through this list of "good" habits and add any others that are relevant to you.

- Know what you need to save to retire and track your progress.

- Make conscious choices about where you spend money.

- Contribute to your RRSP every month of every year.

- Contribute your tax refund to your RRSP every year.

- Be aware of investment returns on retirement savings.

- Have a simple system to keep your retirement plan organized.

- Increase your RRSP contributions every year.

- Engage in periodic conversations about retirement savings with your spouse and family.

- Meet with your financial advisor in person once a year.

- Flip through the *Moolala Guide to Rockin' Your RRSP* once per year as a reminder.

- Recalculate your retirement nest egg every year and check your progress.

**CHOOSE:** What is one retirement savings habit that you are committed to ingraining?

_____

**COMMIT:** Jot down the two or three actions you will take to change the habit.

_____

**TALK:** Tell one other person about the habit that you are committed to changing and the actions you are going to take to do it. Ask them to check in with you every month or so to see how it is going.

The person I'm going to talk with about my new good habit is

_____.

## Conclusion

A habit is a pattern of behaviour and that pattern can be reset if you focus on it. Easier said than done, of course. But I believe it is worth investing both the time and the energy to ingrain habits that help you get a handle on your retirement savings. (If I didn't believe it, then this would be a really stupid book, and a waste of my time to have written it. And I'm not in the habit of wasting time.)

Building knowledge in the area of retirement savings is important and so is developing some skills, but the big idea is to ingrain habits that eliminate the need for detailed project management or great willpower. Next I want to focus on one of the simplest and most effective habits of all: contributing to your RRSP every month of every year.

## { 14 }

## AUTOMATE YOUR
## RETIREMENT SAVINGS
SIGN IT AND FORGET IT

---

I'VE ALWAYS been suspicious of people who do their Christmas shopping year-round. It seems to me that there are better things to do in September than troll the back-to-school sales looking for stocking stuffers. But when it comes to RRSPs, it is actually far easier to contribute year-round than to have to line up with the stressed-out masses every February. I mean, imagine if you had to save up and scramble every spring to get an entire year's worth of mortgage payments together in one day?

### Every Month of Every Year: The Rewards of Regularity

One of the easiest ways to get into the habit of saving for your retirement is to automate the process by setting up a pre-authorized contribution so you contribute every month of every year. The contribution happens regardless of your memory, your mood, or your willpower. It actually takes advantage of human inertia because once you set it, you can forget about it. Here's an endorsement from the Moolala Community:

*"I now put away 10% of my income each month, no matter what the bills add up to. I have it set up as an automatic transfer at the bank, and while it totally sucks that the money just disappears, it really works. It is way easier than making my annual RRSP contribution in one lump sum days before the deadline and I love seeing that account growing each and every month."*

—Corrine, 50, fundraiser. Married with two kids.

**EXERCISE**    ## Set Up a Pre-Authorized Contribution

**REMIND:** You figured out how much you can contribute in chapter 9, taking into account both what the CRA says you are *allowed* and what your cash flow says you can *afford*. Remind yourself of that annual number.

**CALCULATE:** Now divide that annual amount by twelve to calculate a monthly number. Determine if you have enough money to contribute that amount each month. If you do, great. And if you don't, choose a smaller number that will work based on your financial reality. Then stay tuned for the section on "sustainable spending" coming up in chapter 15.

**AUTHORIZE:** Now you just need to arrange for that amount to be transferred out of your bank account and into your RRSP. Ideally, you will synchronize the transfer with your payday so you don't even notice the money has come and gone. I'm not so deluded to think that you aren't going to miss the money—you might. But it will be worth it.

Call your bank or credit union or visit them online to set up a pre-authorized contribution, even if it's only $100 a month in the beginning. You can change the contribution amount with a quick phone call or click of the mouse, but at least you're changing a habit,

which is hugely important. And $100 represents about ten lunches at the food court or one fancy latte every day for a month. I'll be honest and say that $100 a month likely won't likely be enough for your ideal retirement, but it is a start.

Oh, and when I say, "call your bank to authorize the automatic transfer," I mean like right now. Put down this book, and call them. Right. Now. Then tick one of these two boxes.

☐ I have set up an automatic transfer.

☐ I have not set up an automatic transfer, but I promise I will in the next twenty-four hours.

## Feast or Famine: RRSPs for those with volatile income

The reality for many people in today's economy is that income can fluctuate wildly month to month: freelancers, consultants, commissioned sales reps, actors, artists, writers—these professionals can earn solid income, but with almost no consistency. You can barely plan to be at your own wedding with certainty, let alone plan for regular retirement savings. Here are a few things you can do to manage the ups and downs.

### Save a percentage of every cheque:
### One for me, one for my future

A monthly pre-authorized transfer to your RRSP? That is just not going to work when you have volatile income. Instead, contribute a percentage of every cheque you receive to your retirement savings. You probably do something similar for your taxes (at least I hope you do, so you don't develop a bleeding ulcer every year when it comes time to pay your tax bill). The money sitting in your bank account for taxes isn't yours—it belongs to the government. It might help to think about your retirement savings as someone else's money as well, except that person is your future self. And your future self will need that money desperately when you are 80 years old. So for every cheque you receive, put away money for taxes payable in a separate account and do the same with your retirement savings. Start with 10% if you can. I know that might be a stretch, but see what you can do to increase that percentage over time.

**Live on a "fixed" income:**
**Pretending your paycheque is predictable**

Look at your last three years of income after taxes, then "fix" your income and expenditures, including your retirement savings. Put all your income into a savings account and then make two monthly transfers: the first goes to a chequing account for your rent, gro-ceries, and incidentals, and is the same amount every month; the second goes to your RRSP, and is also the same amount every month. During higher-income periods you'll build up a surplus in the savings account, and in lower income periods you'll draw on the surplus.

**Avoid lifestyle inflation: Save more as you make more**

After months of living off ramen noodles like a 22-year-old, you *finally* receive the cheque that was months in the earning. Sure, have a little feast, but be careful to avoid what is called "lifestyle inflation." That refers to what can happen when you have more money than usual in your wallet: you get used to spending it, instead of increasing the amount you put into savings. While it is difficult to keep a cap on lifestyle inflation, it is much more difficult to rein in spending once you get used to spending money.

## Automate Your Tax Refund:
## Contribute It Back to Your RRSP Every Year

Another good habit that will help you automate your RRSP is to con-tribute your tax refund back to your RRSP every year, regardless of whether you have a constant income or a volatile one. I know that cheque feels like a nice windfall for good deeds done, but it isn't. It is money that the government was borrowing interest-free from you for a while and now is giving back. Instead of blowing it on Cuba, cars, or cosmetics, transfer it to your RRSP right away, every year. Aside from paying off credit card debt, this is one of the best uses for that money. You'll get the tax deduction and your money will have a chance to grow tax-deferred for years, becoming a nice nest egg to help fund your activities in retirement.

## Conclusion

Use the power of human enertia to your benefit. Automating your retirement savings will get you what you want faster and more easily than if you have to think about it every year. Another thing that will make a big difference is increasing your RRSP contribution over time. I know. I know. You can't have two spare nickels to rub together. But hear me out. Flip the page to learn more about sustainable spending.

# { 15 }

## INCREASE THE AMOUNT
## OF YOUR RRSP CONTRIBUTION
### IMPROVE YOUR CASH FLOW
### TO HELP YOU SAVE MORE

---

**Y**OU HAVE successfully opened up an RRSP account, found some money to contribute to it, invested that money in some combination of fixed income and equity, and perhaps even set up a regular pre-authorized contribution. It is now time to work on increasing your contribution. I know. You might be thinking, "Cut me some slack. Can't we just celebrate what I have accomplished?"

Yes, we can. For a minute.

Hooray! Go you.

And now we are gracefully moving on to how you can increase the amount of your RRSP contribution.

While the government determines how much you are *allowed* to put into your RRSP every year, it's up to you, of course, to determine how much you can *afford* to contribute. If you're like most Canadians, you have lots of contribution room sitting there. And in the absence of an inheritance, lottery win, or excellent night at the blackjack table, there is likely only one way you're going to be able to max it out: improve your cash flow.

## Sustainable Spending:
## The ABCs of Changing Your Spending Stripes

You bring in a certain amount of income every year, and you have a bunch of expenses that eat up that income. The difference between income and expenses is called cash flow. It can be either positive or negative. If you notice your outstanding credit card balance is going up, you can bet that you have a negative cash flow.

In order to increase your RRSP contribution, you'll likely have to improve your cash flow by increasing your income, cutting your expenses, or doing a bit of both. Here's my tried and true ABC strategy for what I call "sustainable spending": Analyze, Brainstorm, and Change.

**EXERCISE** Sing the ABCs
With Your Money

I cover sustainable spending in more detail in *Moolala,* but have outlined the basic process here. I've got some worksheets to help you do this analysis, available for free on moolala.ca.

**ANALYZE:** Where is your money coming from and going to? Grab your credit card and bank statements and calculate how much money is coming in and how much is going towards your mortgage or rent, food, transportation, entertainment, pets, hobbies et cetera. You'll probably be able to download the data from your online banking into Excel if you're really keen, but keep the complexity of this analysis to a minimum. You might be surprised at how much you spend in some areas, or how little you really know about where your money goes. Jot down a few insights here:

_____

_____

**BRAINSTORM:** Now that you have a sense of what is currently going on with your cash flow, think about what you could do differently that would increase your income or cut your spending.

_____

_____

This is the time to get creative: for example, you could get a room-mate, work a second job, cancel cable, pack your lunch, sell your car or vinyl collection or wedding dress. Put down some ideas here, even if they seem a little far-fetched at this point.

_____

_____

**COMMIT:** What are the changes you're willing to commit to that will make the biggest difference to your financial situation? Choose two or three changes that you will commit to.

_____

_____

Working on sustainable spending for a few hours once or twice a year can reap big rewards and help you get a handle on your money so you can live the life you want.

## Conclusion

I am not a fan of frugality—life is too short to count every last penny. But I am a big believer in sustainable spending—setting up your life so you make a few big, conscious choices about your money and then don't have to think about it every five minutes. The exercise above likely highlighted some habits that you might want to change. Up next are some tips and tricks for turning bad habits into good ones.

# { 16 }

## GOOD THINGS COME TO
## THOSE WHO WAIT

### LEAVE YOUR RRSPS TO
### GROW IN PEACE

---

STAYING ENGAGED is the final step of the Moolala Method and it is much simpler to do when you have good retirement savings habits. But even as good as those habits are, sometimes you get thrown off by some sort of external event: a new baby, a divorce, a job loss or a death in the family. Or a big decline in the stock market could make you wonder if investing your money was such a good idea after all. But before you consider withdrawing money from your RRSP to help deal with a crisis in your life, or a crisis of confidence, consider two big downsides.

The first is that you will pay tax on the money you withdraw because it is now deemed to be "income." If you're unemployed, for example, and have dropped to a lower tax bracket, that will be less of an issue than if you're still earning your full salary. But that is likely money you'd prefer not to pay out right now. And secondly, if you take money out of your RRSP it won't be there for you in the future. I know that sounds blindingly obvious, but you're trading off having the money today with having money in the future when your 80-year-old self could really use it.

Some people would say that a job loss is a good reason to withdraw from an RRSP. I would argue that doing so should be the last resort as it will be so difficult to get caught up. That said, if you are close to retirement and you have no income it might make sense. The bottom line is that any decision about withdrawing from your RRSP needs to be taken with your whole financial picture in mind, and your picture is unique to you. See the sidebars for examples from people considering taking money out of their RRSPs and what I have to say about it.

## How Painful Will It Be If I Withdraw from My RRSP Early?

**QUESTION:**

*"I have lost my job and want to withdraw $15,000 from my RRSP to cover my expenses. The bank told me that they will take away $3,000 and give me $12,000 and a T4. My income was around $45,000 per year and I am single. Approximately how much tax will I be paying for that extra $15,000?"*

**ANSWER:**

Cashing in a portion of your RRSP is painful. It's supposed to be. All the better to discourage you from taking your money out instead of keeping it invested until retirement. But it sounds like you really need access to that cash, and, as painful as it is, you now have to face the tax implications of withdrawing money from your RRSP.

### Paying tax on RRSP withdrawals

A number of variables will impact how much income tax you will end up paying on the $15,000 you are going to withdraw, for example, which province you live in, the source of the income and other tax deductions you may have.

A rough number for the actual tax you would owe on this tax return when reporting the RRSP withdrawal is about 30%, or $4,500. So the $3,000 of tax the bank will withhold is just a pre-payment of some of the tax. Banks are required to withhold a certain percentage of the withdrawal—20%, or $3,000 in this case.

### Exploring other options

It sounds like you were taken aback by the amount of tax the bank told you they would withhold. This makes me wonder if you've explored other avenues. You are going to withdraw $15,000 from your RRSP, but because of the tax, keep only $10,500 of it. How else could you come up with that amount?

If you own your home, could you refinance the mortgage? Do you have investments outside of your RRSP? If you do, could you cash them in instead? Do you have a line of credit, or is there a family member who could loan you the money? Do you have any other assets that you could sell?

I don't know anything about your situation, but it is also worth reconsidering whether this really is an emergency. For example, the car breaks down and you need transportation to get to and from work. But is a new car an emergency? Or is there a way you could get by on public transit or by buying an inexpensive used car to get you back on the road. This $15,000 isn't just $15,000. If you are able to find another way to deal with your current financial crisis and keep that money invested it will grow into a much bigger number—$122,000, if you keep it invested for 35 years and make just 6% on it.

All that said, withdrawing from your RRSP might really be your only option. You shouldn't make a habit of RRSP withdrawals, but sometimes people fall on tough times and you shouldn't feel guilty about having to make tough decisions.

It sounds like a tough decision. Best of luck to you in making it.

 ## Should We Sell Some of Our RRSPs to Pay for Diapers?

**QUESTION:**

*"My wife and I are expecting our first child in a few months. We currently have a combined income of about $150,000, but we are struggling with how to manage financially while she is on*

*maternity leave. That's because we are carrying $19,000 in credit card debt and have been putting $1,300 towards it every two weeks, but that is not going to be an option once the baby arrives. I currently have $24,000 in RRSPs and I have begun to wonder if selling them may be a good option to get rid of our credit debt. If we no longer have credit card debt, that would free up about $400 as the minimum payment each month to go towards the mortgage or baby expenses. Is this a smart idea?"*

**ANSWER:**

I like that you're thinking outside of the box and working on getting your financial house in order before your baby arrives. But selling your RRSPs to pay down credit card debt is not the way to do it, for two main reasons: math and discipline.

### Cashing in RRSPs will trigger a big tax bill

I understand your thinking. You have a big credit card debt in one hand and more than enough money to eliminate it in the other. Except for one problem. That money is sitting in an RRSP, and if you cash it out you will trigger a big tax bill. Basically the government will say that you have earned that $24,000 in income and will tax you on it, just as if you got a juicy bonus at work.

For simplicity, let's say your tax rate is 40%. That means you'll pay $9,600 when you file your income taxes, leaving you with just $14,400 to put towards the credit card debt. So you'll incur a huge tax hit and you still won't have enough money to pay off the debt.

### Compound interest turns pennies into gold

I know it is going to be tough to protect the money inside your RRSP. But don't think of it as just $24,000. Think of it as $194,000. Because that is what it will be worth if you leave it in there and let compound interest turn those pennies into gold at 6% for the next thirty-five years.

Sure, your credit card debt is costing you more in interest than you earn on your RRSP investments—probably 25% versus 6%. But the compound interest calculation underscores the importance of letting your retirement savings grow and finding another way to eliminate the bathtub full of credit card debt you're dragging along with you.

### Having a baby isn't an emergency

I can understand why some people have no other choice than to cash out their RRSP. They are dealing with some sort of health or family emergency and this is their last resort. But a new baby is not an emergency and cashing out your RRSP to provide for one undermines the discipline of saving for your retirement.

You make good money as a family, and while these next two years are going to be lean financially, you will be able to get back on track much faster than someone who earns less. It is stressful, but take the long view. Stay disciplined and protect your retirement savings.

Now that you've heard my sermon on protecting your RRSP, here are three actions I suggest you take to improve your situation.

1. **Find another lender:** I get a little nauseous thinking of you paying 25% interest on your $19,000 credit card debt, so I can imagine how upsetting that must be for you every month. You need to try to find another lender that will charge you a lower interest rate. Even if you have already tried to do this, try again. Take your pregnant wife with you to the bank. That should warm up even the coldest-hearted banker. Your combined household income is very good, and banks have some latitude to make exceptions. Ask them what your options are. Do you qualify for a loan for even part of the total amount? Can you use real estate to secure a line of credit? Is there a family member you could ask to co-sign a loan at the bank? Could that family member lend you the money directly?

2. **Exercise restraint on baby spending:** I know you'll probably roll your eyes at this one. But I recommend you exercise restraint on baby spending. Sure, it can be really expensive. But for the

most part, it doesn't have to be, especially in the first year. You will not need $400 a month for baby expenses. As the father of a three-year-old I have been subjected to the intense marketing and societal guilt that is focused on new parents. You and your wife may *want* lots of things for your baby in its first year, but there is very little that you actually *need*: a crib, a car seat, some onesies, and diapers. Most of this stuff can come from the local thrift shop, online sites like Kijiji, or loans from friends and family. Put the word out to a few friends that you'd prefer them to come together to buy you a car seat instead of other baby gifts.

3. **Build up cash reserves now:** You still have a bit of time before the baby is born. I would also look at what else you could cut from your spending now: cable, cell phones, eating out, et cetera. As you will soon discover, you can't build up your reserves of sleep, unfortunately. But you can build up your reserves of cash. Enjoy the ride.

## How Do I Deal With the Stock Market Roller Coaster?

**QUESTION:**

*"When there is turmoil and significant volatility in the TSX, my investment advisor continually says to stay the course. In 2008 the index was at 15,000, then dropped to 7,500 and still has not recovered. I'm 45 years old. My portfolio is 50% equity, 50% fixed income, invested in low-cost mutual funds. Do you support my adviser's position on this?"*

**ANSWER:**

Yes. I do support your adviser's position and believe that it is critical to stay the course in periods of market volatility. One of the biggest mistakes the average investor can make is getting caught in the violent and ever-changing current of the stock market. They can get greedy as the markets climb, then panic when they fall, as if surprised by the volatility. But volatility isn't a surprise. The stock market is volatile—that is how it behaves. For example, the TSX is up about 9.5% per year over the past 50 years, but it has seen huge dips along the way—during the crash of 1987, the Asian crisis in 1998, the dot-com bust in 2000, the terrorist attacks in 2001, and the financial meltdown in 2008. If you had sold your position during any of these periods and stayed out of the market, you would have missed out on significant gains as the market rebounded.

All that being said, there are some additional questions you should be reviewing with your advisor that may or may not lead you to change your asset allocation away from equity. But you should do this based on your goals and not the day-to-day volatility of the market.

- **What is your nest egg for?** Talk through your goals again with your advisor to ensure that you're still singing from the same song sheet. Is your goal to simply fund your retirement? Or do you want to leave a legacy for your family? It may be that moving to 100% fixed income will impair your ability to meet your goals, or it may not. Talk that through.

- **How does a worst-case scenario really affect you?** Based on those goals, what happens if the TSX drops back to 5,000? Does it make you feel bad? Or does it impact your ability to buy groceries? For a 40-year-old like me, a 50% decline in the stock market is a loss on paper only. It is hard to stomach, of course, but it doesn't impact my ability to pay for groceries during retirement because I still have a lot of time to wait for markets to recover. That is why I'm only marginally interested in these gyrations—I'm not trying to time the market so they aren't relevant to me. Have your advisor show you the numbers and see if you can live with the consequences of the worst-case scenario.

- **Has your risk tolerance changed?** Your asset allocation is about right for your age, using the rule of thumb of fixed income to age. But something may have changed in your circumstances or mindset that would make you want to lower your risk. Ponder this and talk to your advisor about it.

- **What would be the strategy to lower your equity stake?** If your risk tolerance has changed, or this new discussion about your goals leads to a reduction in your equity stake, ask your advisor for a recommendation on how to do it over time, instead of pushing the panic button right now. For example, you might have shares that you bought at $22 that you could sell now at $40. You'd be reducing your equity position, but still at a profit, even though the shares are off their high.

Let's be clear: you have a choice. You don't have to invest in the stock market. However, if you choose to get out, do it because your goals have changed, not because of the market. It is doing what it has always done—going up and down, keeping people awake at night and providing endless fodder for financial pundits who believe they can figure out when the stock market is about to rise or fall.

## Conclusion

Staying engaged with your retirement savings is difficult at the best of times, let alone when life throws you a curveball. But if you find your resolve slipping, go back to the very beginning—to your context for your retirement savings. Remind yourself why you're doing all this work in the first place. My retirement savings are for adventure. And while the process sometimes totally sucks, that remains a compelling motivation for me.

We are almost at end of the *Moolala Guide to Rockin' Your RRSP*. There is only one more thing to cover: a checklist to bring together everything that we have been working on.

# { 17 }

## BRING IT ALL TOGETHER

### COMPLETE THE CHECKLIST
### TO ROCK YOUR RRSPS

---

WE HAVE covered a lot of ground in the *Moolala Guide to Rockin' Your* RRSP. Some of it might have been a really tough, upward climb for you, but the end of our trek is in sight. Before we plunk down in front of the fire at our campsite with our beverage of choice in hand, I'd like to take a few minutes to bring all that we have covered together in one place.

I am one of those people who feel a tremendous amount of satisfaction crossing items off a list. You might be like me, or you might be repelled by the thought of a checklist for your retirement savings. Love it or hate it, the final exercise of this guide is a checklist you can use to track your actions. A printable version can be downloaded at moolala.ca.

**EXERCISE**    **Complete the Moolala RRSP Checklist**

Now, those of you who have been doing the exercises all along and taking action as you worked through the guide will move fairly quickly through the checklist. And those of you who haven't been quite so keen will have some catching up to do. You know who you are. And I know who you are.

**COMPLETE:** Work your way through the checklist below, adding a satisfying "√" when you have completed the task. You won't likely complete the checklist in one swoop, so keep it handy to update as you move through it.

### The Moolala RRSP checklist

| STEP 1: LAY THE FOUNDATION |
| :--- |
| ☐ Create a context: When it comes to retirement, what is money for? |
| ☐ Brainstorm activities you might take on in retirement |
| ☐ Identify the consequences of your behaviour around retirement savings |
| ☐ Review the basic "who, what, when, where, why and how" of RRSPs |
| **STEP 2: DETERMINE HOW MUCH YOU NEED** |
| ☐ Consult an online retirement calculator |
| ☐ Check to see whether your nest egg is on track |
| **STEP 3: DEVELOP THE PLAN** |
| ☐ Articulate your retirement goal |
| ☐ Choose a retirement savings vehicle |
| ☐ Determine how much you can contribute |
| **STEP 4: TAKE ACTION** |
| ☐ Identify your hurdle to taking action |
| ☐ Identify what it will take for you to take action |
| ☐ Open up an RRSP and contribute to it |
| ☐ Determine what to invest your contribution in |
| **STEP 5: STAY ENGAGED** |
| ☐ Improve your "good" habits one at a time |
| ☐ Set up a pre-authorized contribution |
| ☐ Increase the amount of your RRSP contribution |
| ☐ Leave your RRSPs to grow in peace |
| ☐ Complete the Moolala RRSP checklist again every year |

## Conclusion

You started the *Moolala Guide to Rockin' Your* RRSP by laying the foundation for your retirement and then determined how much you would need to pay for it. You followed that by developing a plan for your retirement savings and then taking action on it. You are now in the "staying engaged" phase, the fifth and final step of the Moolala Method.

Staying engaged does not mean poring over your mutual statements every month or paying attention to the minute-by-minute moves on the stock market. This step is about ingraining a few key habits that will help ensure the money is there for what you want to do in retirement.

I have been focused on doing three things throughout this guide. First, to make retirement savings relevant to you and your life. This was why I was so focused on your identifying your context for retirement savings and brainstorming some activities you'd like to do when your time is your own. The second thing was to have you develop a simple plan to rock your RRSPs immediately. The checklist you just completed is that plan—and I trust that it is enough to get you moving. And the third thing was to inspire you to get off your duff and take action. The Moolala Community is made up of people just like you. They have similar dreams, strengths and weaknesses, and good and bad habits, and I hope their examples have given you some confidence in your own ability to get a handle on your retirement savings.

With that, I turn it over to you. Go out and take action.

Perhaps we'll see each other in a few decades in the mountains of Patagonia. God willing, I'll be the guy laughing hysterically in my little tent with my adult daughter at my side.

> **Staying engaged does not mean poring over your mutual statements every month or paying attention to the minute-by-minute moves on the stock market.**

# BORROWING FROM YOUR RRSP

## THE HOME BUYERS' PLAN AND LIFELONG LEARNING PLAN

---

O NE GREAT benefit of building up your RRSP is that you can borrow from it to buy or build your first home or continue your education. The Home Buyers' Plan (HBP) and the Lifelong Learning Plan (LLP) allow you to withdraw money from your RRSP without paying tax on it, subject to certain limits and conditions. You do have to pay the money back within a set period of time, but the plans might give you some wiggle room to fund some goals you want to achieve now, rather than in thirty years from now. So if you just can't imagine starting to save for your retirement, but could see yourself needing the down payment for a house, or tuition money for an MBA, here is another good reason to sock money away in an RRSP.

### Upping Your Down Payment with The Home Buyers' Plan

Home prices have been rocketing towards Mars for years now, making it very difficult for a first-time home buyer to save for a down payment. If you have been putting something away in your RRSP for a few years, you may have part of your down payment right there. As long as you and your potential new nest meet the conditions set out by the federal government, the Home Buyers' Plan will allow you to withdraw up to $25,000 from your RRSP, penalty-free, to put towards the purchase of your first home. That is a much better option than selling a kidney.

The government expects you to repay the amount you withdrew from your RRSP within fifteen years (think of it as a long-term, interest-free loan to yourself). You don't get a deduction for the repayment and must repay a minimum amount to your RRSP each year of the fifteen-year repayment period, though you can repay more. But whatever you *don't* pay back in any given year must be declared as income, and will be taxed accordingly. Ouch. And if you don't repay the money you lose that contribution room forever. Double Ouch. You must start repaying the amount you withdrew beginning in the second year following the year you made the withdrawal. As a friendly reminder the Canada Revenue Agency will send you a handy notice of assessment to ensure you know how much you have to repay each year. It's obviously to your great benefit to get that money back into your RRSP so it and the interest it earns will be waiting for you when you retire.

Full details are available on the CRA website. But here's a primer on the conditions for qualifying for the HBP:

- You must be a first-time home buyer. Pretty straightforward, although this condition doesn't apply if you are a person with a disability or you are buying or building a home for a relative with a disability. You can in fact participate in the HBP more than once, but not if you or your spouse or common-law partner owned a home within a four-year period of the calendar year you intend to make the withdrawal, and not until you have repaid the balance borrowed from your RRSP under the HBP the previous time.

- Your RRSP contributions must remain in the RRSP for at least ninety days before you can withdraw the money under the HBP. (Just don't do any fancy withdrawing from your RRSP for other reasons in the three-month period leading up to the date of your withdrawal.)

- You must be a resident of Canada, and the home you want to buy must be located in Canada. (Yup, you're on your own when it comes to buying that little piece of paradise in Costa Rica.)

- You can take the HBP money out in bits but, ultimately, the entire amount you want to borrow must be withdrawn within the same calendar year.

- If you and your spouse or common-law partner wish to participate in the HBP together, both of you need to qualify as first-time home buyers before you can each withdraw money from your individual RRSPs under the HBP.

- You must intend to live in the home within one calendar year of purchasing it. This is important to know if you're buying a condo that might take a long time to build, or if you were hoping to use the HBP for a rental property.

- There is no penalty from the government's perspective, but there may be a penalty from your financial institution. For example, if you have mutual funds you may be hit with a deferred sales charge (DSC) when you sell them.

~~~~~~~~~~~~~~~~~~~~~~~~~~~~~~~~~~~~~~~~~~~~~~~~~~~~~~~~~~

 **Should We Repay Our Home Buyers' Plan Loan?**

**QUESTION:**

*"My husband and I are both in our 30s and withdrew from our RRSPs under the first-time home buyers' plan. Our question is whether it is worth it for us to pay off the HBP loan, which is about $35,000 between us. His parents say that having an RRSP is useless, because it only lowers the pension amount that we can get when we retire. My husband has a pension plan as a federal government employee and I have one through my work at a hospital. My husband earns $60,000 per year, while I earn $39,000. Money is a bit tight right now as we are trying to pay off more of*

*our mortgage every month and I just found out today that I'm four
weeks' pregnant. We are so confused about whether to pay more
on our mortgage, buy RRSPs, or pay off our HBP. Please guide us on
what to do."*

**ANSWER:**

In-laws are great. They have a never-ending supply of embarrassing
stories from your husband's past, and if they live nearby, perhaps
they will provide some child care for you in the future. (Congrats on
the baby news, by the way.) But in-laws don't necessarily provide
the best financial advice, as you pointed out in your question.

### RRSPs won't affect pension income

Your husband's parents told you that an RRSP would lower the pension amount you get when you retire. But neither of these pensions
are "means-tested." That is, they don't have anything to do with
your other sources of income. Perhaps your in-laws were thinking
about Old Age Security, which does get clawed back if your income
exceeds a certain level. But given that it will be thirty years before
you start collecting OAS, it is impossible to say what the program
will actually look like and how much you'll be able to draw from it.
So it makes the most sense to focus on things that will provide the
best life for you post-retirement.

As for the claim that RRSPs are "useless," I beg to differ. RRSPs
are a great way to save for retirement because they allow you to
defer income tax into the future. This is less critical for you than for
many people because you and your husband both have pensions,
but it is still a big benefit. It is true that you'll have to pay more taxes
if you have RRSPs than someone who doesn't have them. But that
is because you have *income* to pay for things and the other person
doesn't!

### Unpaid HBP loans treated as taxable income

If you choose not to repay the HBP loan, the government will treat
the amount as income and you'll have to pay tax on it, either by

writing a bigger cheque to Canada Revenue Agency or receiving a lower tax refund. Ouch.

### HBP loan should be the focus instead of additional mortgage repayment

You also mentioned that you were trying to pay as much as you can on your mortgage. If mortgage rates were at 20%, that would be the right approach. But rates are at historic lows, so it makes more sense to pay back your HBP and avoid the tax hit than to avoid the 3% to 5% interest you're paying on your mortgage. Generally speaking you need to repay one-fifteenth of the $35,000 amount you withdrew under the HBP every year. That works out to just under $200 per month. My advice would be to stop trying to pay more on your mortgage and instead focus on your HBP repayment.

If you're anything like we were, you are probably wildly excited and totally stressed about the arrival of a child. If you really can't repay both of your HBP loans simultaneously, focus on your husband's first because he is in the higher tax bracket.

### You're doing better than you think you are

If the only debt you have right now is your mortgage, you're doing really well for a young couple. If you had a big chunk of credit card debt I'd be more inclined to ignore the HBP repayments, but you don't have consumer debt, and you do have pensions. You would be amazed how many people would give anything to trade places with you.

~~~~~~~~~~~~~~~~~~~~~~~~~~~~~~~~~

### Investing in education with the Lifelong Learning Plan

Going back to school could be the fulfillment of a dream for you, or it could be a big investment in your current career or in an entirely new one. If a master's degree in leadership or a diploma in cabinet-making is your goal, the Lifelong Learning Plan (LLP) might be your ticket to achieve it.

Here's how it works: the LLP allows you to withdraw money from an RRSP to attend a "qualifying education program"—or to fund the educational dream of your spouse or common-law partner. Under the LLP, you can withdraw a maximum annual amount of $10,000 from your RRSP to a total limit of $20,000 for the period you are participating in the LLP, as long as you meet the following conditions:

• You must be a full-time student and resident of Canada.

• You must be enrolled, or have received an offer to enrol in your program of choice before March of the year after you withdraw the money.

• You must choose a qualifying educational program at a designated educational institute (check out the CRA website or give them a call to make sure).

Similar to the HBP, the LLP requires that you repay the borrowed amount within a certain time frame—in the case of the LLP, that's ten years. If you don't, you'll be taxed on the amount you owe for the year as if it's income. Again, it's in your best interest to pay the money back so you can continue to grow your retirement nest egg, tax-deferred.

The schedule for paying back the amount into your RRSP will show up in an LLP statement of account that you'll receive every year; generally speaking, your repayments will start the fifth year after your first LLP withdrawal. (Note: you've got to get things squared away with repayments before the end of the year you turn 71—just think of how smart you'll be by then.)

If you take the phrase "lifelong learner" to heart and you (or your spouse or common-law partner) decide to go back to school yet again, you'll be happy to know that you can participate in the LLP as many times as you like—you just have to wait until one year after you've paid back the amount you first borrowed.

# APPENDIX B

# POST-RRSP LIFE:

## LOOKING AHEAD TO AGE 71

YOU MAY be years or even decades from emptying your wine cellar. But at some point you'll retire, or at least partly retire. You'll need access to the money that you so carefully accumulated in that wine cellar over the past few decades. The money you withdraw is considered income and will be taxed at your current marginal tax rate. But you can't keep your RRSP open indefinitely.

Age 71 (which, according to boomer-lifestyle magazines, is the new 51) is a pivotal year for those with RRSPs. By December 31 of your 71st year, federal regulations require that you terminate your RRSP (maybe don't wait until New Year's Eve to get on that; you'll have better things to do) and make a decision about the next stage for your investments.

A detailed discussion about your post-RRSP options is outside the scope of this book. But here is a super simple overview:

• **Establishing a RRIF.** A Registered Retirement Income Fund, or RRIF, is like an RRSP in some ways. It is also an account that holds investments that you'll use to fund your life in retirement, and those investments continue to grow tax-deferred. But instead of putting *in* money up to a maximum amount every year as with an RRSP, a RRIF requires that holders take a minimum amount of money *out* every year. An RRSP is about asset accumulation while a RRIF is about slow and steady asset depletion. What's great about the RRIF is that, just like an RRSP, you won't be taxed on the money in your RRIF, only on the amount you withdraw every year. Most people establish a RRIF close to age 71, but you are allowed to convert your RRSP earlier if you'd like.

- **Purchasing a Fixed Term Annuity or Life Annuity.** This entails handing your entire investment over to a life insurance company that will then guarantee you a set monthly income for an agreed number of years. You won't have to worry about stock market stability or investing, you'll just get the same income month in and month out. If you die before all the payments are received, what's left goes to your estate.

- **Cashing out the entire RRSP.** To put it mildly, this is generally a very bad idea as you'll have to include the entire amount withdrawn as taxable income, thus taking a tax hit on all your hard-earned savings. That will make you cry.

## Is It a Good Idea to Cash in Our RRSPs?

**QUESTION:**

*"An insurance salesman/investment adviser recently suggested that since my wife is currently a homemaker with no income, we should withdraw her RRSPs a little each year and invest that money in a non-registered account with him. Since the withdrawal amount would be just below the threshold for income tax and my wife has essentially no other income, no taxes would be owed. It has been drilled into me that you shouldn't touch RRSPs until retirement or unless absolutely necessary. In fact, I asked our current portfolio manager about this and he is dead set against it. Is this a good idea?"*

**ANSWER:**

No. In my opinion this is not a good idea. While he is not incorrect on the tax implications, I can't see how this would be a good idea for you. Here's why:

### "Don't touch your RRSPs unless absolutely necessary"

As you say, you have had the "don't touch" philosophy drilled into you. The main reason for that—aside from the risk of triggering a tax bill—is because it protects you from yourself. Having your retirement savings in a registered plan makes it harder to access the money and therefore harder to spend. Some people choose to borrow from their RRSPs, to help them buy a home or pay for education, but they have to pay that money back. Withdrawing the money to invest is folly.

### Don't let the taxman "touch" it either

Income earned on money in a non-registered account will be taxed. But if that money is held in a registered retirement savings plan, it can grow without being taxed, until it is withdrawn. True, your wife can withdraw a little each year from her RRSP and avoid an income tax hit, but whatever those new investments earn in the non-registered account will be taxable. And besides, you, as her husband, will receive a "spousal tax credit" because your wife has no income. If she withdraws from her RRSP you will lose this credit and ultimately pay the tax.

Remember that an RRSP is intended for *retirement*, not to supplement low-income years while you're raising your kids.

# ACKNOWLEDGEMENTS

I AM GRATEFUL TO the many people who provided insight and support in the creation of this book. Jesse Finkelstein and Trena White at Page Two Strategies, Chris Labonté and everyone at Figure 1 Publishing, and the fantastic folks at Raincoast Books all worked under crazy pressure to hit our ambitious deadline.

I am grateful to the many people who gave me feedback on the various drafts. Matthew Ardrey, Dean Paley, Jim Yih, Melanie Jeannotte, Paul Gomery, and Beth Hamilton-Keen found time to help, despite their frenetic jobs in the financial industry. Jeanne LeSage, Janis Auster, Donna Bishop, and Larcina Abbott represented the smart, inspiring readers this book was written for and suggested many ways to make the book more relevant and readable.

Anita Chong, Jacqueline Moore, and Mark Brown also contributed invaluable editorial insight along the way. And the many, many members of the Moolala Community provided their specific stories that you see peppered throughout the book.

As the parent of a toddler, I am grateful to those who helped me find time to write and treated our daughter as a member of their families. Thanks to Deb Hagen, Diane Hinds, Julie Hamilton, and Kelly Raffan.

And finally, I want to thank my daughter, Abby, for being a fountain of joy in our lives, and my husband, Dennis, for being my number one fan.

DAVID COOPER

**BRUCE SELLERY** is author of the *Globe and Mail* bestselling book *Moolala: Why Smart People Do Dumb Things with Their Money (and What You Can Do About It)*. He is a columnist for *MoneySense*, Canada's personal finance magazine, and a regular contributor on CBC-TV's *The Lang & O'Leary Exchange*. Bruce hosted *Million Dollar Neighbourhood* on the Oprah Winfrey Network and was one of the founding staff members of CTV's Business News Network. He is a member of the Canadian Association of Professional Speakers and an alumnus of the Governor General's Leadership Conference. He earned an Honours Bachelor of Commerce degree from the Queen's School of Business in Kingston, Ontario, and, prior to his move into business journalism was a brand manager at Procter & Gamble. He lives with his family in Toronto, Ontario.